L.D. FROM THE INSIDE OUT

by

Carolyn Lampman Brubaker

Please return to:
Parents Helping Parents of Wy. Inc.
500 W. Lott St, Suite A
Buffalo, WY 82834
1-800-660-9742

WHISKEY CREEK PRESS
www.whiskeycreekpress.com

Published by
WHISKEY CREEK PRESS

Whiskey Creek Press
PO Box 51052
Casper, WY 82605-1052
www.whiskeycreekpress.com

Copyright © 2005 by *Carolyn Brubaker*

No part of this book may be reproduced or transmitted in any form or by any means, electronic or mechanical, including photocopying, recording, or by any information storage and retrieval system, without permission in writing from the publisher.

ISBN 1-59374-198-7

Credits:
Cover Artist: Nora Baxter
Editor: Angela Waters

Printed in the United States of America

Dedication

This book is dedicated to everyone who struggles with the hidden "gift" of L.D., especially those who were brave enough to let me tell their stories. You know who you are and how proud I am of each and every one of you!

TABLE OF CONTENTS

Introduction	1
1-L.D. The Hidden Gift	3
2-Reading	13
3-Math	28
4-Oral Language	47
5-Written Language	60
6-Processing Problems, Reasons Johnny Can't Read	73
7-Social Skills	87
8-ADD & ADHD	103
9-Homework	116
10-Chores	132
11-Special Projects	141
12-Gifted L.D	155
13-Preparing Yourself For the IEP meeting	165
14-When Parents and School Disagree	180
15-Resources	194
Glossary	198
APPENDIX 1 P&A and PIC Addresses	205
APPENDIX 2 Impartial Due Process Hearing	257
APPENDIX 3 Parental Rights	270

Introduction

"It's difficult to predict this early, but I'm afraid he's going to have trouble in school." The Kindergarten teacher's words played over and over in my head as I walked out the door after parent teacher conferences. I could feel hot tears pressing against my eyelids; tears I knew were going to spill over any minute and embarrass me. The teacher had been talking about my youngest son, our final hope for a *normal* child. Fifteen minutes before I'd heard almost exactly the same thing, in stronger words from my daughter's second grade teacher.

It wasn't like I'd never heard it before. School personnel had been saying it about my two older sons for eight years. Suddenly the years stretched before me with unbearable heartache as I realized I had another thirteen years of negative conferences ahead of me, in all twenty-one years in which I would *never* hear a positive word about any of my children.

I know many of you reading this book have similar stories. I was lucky. After nineteen years of teaching children with learning disabilities, I knew my own would be all right. I've met adults with learning disabilities in all walks of life including doctors, lawyers, artists, writers, truck drivers, actors, mechanics, and most recently a dyslexic literary agent. Some of my former students have gone on to become business owners, store managers, clerks, secretaries, and even special ED teachers.

On a more personal level, I was born with several learning disabilities of my own. But it doesn't stop there. My husband, our four children, all three of my brothers and an assortment of nieces and nephews on both sides also have learning disabilities. We even have an obese goldfish that swims upside down. In our house, L.D. is normal. Because we are aware of it, we have learned how to cope with it.

Yet, even with all that background and the deep down conviction that my children would eventually become productive adults, my feelings at the end of that parent-teacher conference could only be described as broken-hearted. How much worse for a parent without my experience; the utter hopelessness must be nearly overwhelming.

Thus the idea for this book was born. It is exactly what the title implies, a survival guide, but it is more than that. I hope to change the way you think about learning disabilities, to help you see your child as the unique and intelligent being he or she is.

It's not necessary to read this book cover to cover. Use it as a handbook to guide you in helping your child learn to cope in an unsympathetic world. Use it to reassure yourself that learning disabilities are not fatal. Most importantly, use it to give yourself back the hope of a bright future for your child.

Chapter 1

Learning Disabilities: The Hidden Gift

> With tender loving care,
> All flowers will bloom,
> Each with their own beauty.
> Marge Clark (parent)

In my opinion, the term Learning Disabled is a misnomer. It implies that people with L.D. are unable to learn. Nothing could be further from the truth. By definition, people with L.D. have average or above intelligence. In other words they're smart! So why do they have trouble in school? Quite simply, they learn differently. Of course, that also means they're divergent thinkers, and the world sees that as a positive. It's the reason so many people with learning disabilities are creative, and the reason I refer to L.D. as the hidden gift.

Several years ago my husband attended a meeting for parents of kids with disabilities. The speaker, an 'expert' on learning disabilities, described the child with L.D. as a battery with one dead cell. My husband took instant exception. "No, no," he said, "you have it all wrong. A child with L.D. is like a high performance race car that you don't have tuned just right. Once you find the right combination it will take off and beat all the rest." Truer words were never spoken.

I recently visited an Internet web site for teens with L.D. While there, I discovered a list of eighty-five famous people the media has identified as having L.D. at one time or another.

It is an amazing list of world leaders, inventors, entrepreneurs, athletes, actors, actresses, artists, musicians, generals, comedians, race car drivers, and authors. Personally, I believe the people on that list may well have accomplished their greatness *because* of their learning disabilities, not in spite of them.

Albert Einstein, one of those on the list, said, "Imagination is more important than knowledge." He might well have been talking about L.D. Knowledge is important, of course. It's what man has learned over thousands of years, and almost entirely what we teach in schools. However, all the knowledge in the world can't create anything new. For that you need imagination and divergent thinking, qualities people with learning disabilities tend to have in abundance. That's why I think L.D. should stand for *learns differently* not learning disabled.

Most kids with L.D. walk to the beat of a different drum. Some, like my youngest son Paul, walk to the beat of a different orchestra. Paul is the type of child who gets a building set for Christmas, throws away the directions because he can't read them then proceeds to build a far more complex and imaginative model on his own. As a parent, it is vital that you realize how important your child's unique perspective of the world is. You may not understand it, but you will likely be called upon to nurture and protect that creativity from those who think *different* is somehow bad.

Interestingly enough, if you compare the adult lives of people who were identified either as L.D. or gifted in school, you may discover a strange paradox. As a group, the L.D. population tends to be far more productive and successful in their adult lives than the gifted group.

How could such a thing be true? At first it may seem impossible, but actually the explanation is simple. Our public schools, unfortunately, do not challenge our gifted children. Since everything comes easily to them, they don't know how to handle a challenge and tend to back away from something they can't immediately conquer. Kids with L.D., on the other hand, are challenged every day of their lives. When they run into something new or unusual, they attack it with the same dogged determination that they approach everything else in their lives. Add to that the ability to think differently than the rest of the world, and you have a recipe for success.

No one would dare suggest George Washington, Michelangelo, Charles Darwin, Winston Churchill, Mark Twain, or Napoleon were handicapped. They obviously weren't, and yet each of them appears on the list of famous people with learning disabilities. As an adult with L.D., it has been my personal experience that a learning disability is more of an inconvenience than a handicap. Only when you say, "I can't because I'm L.D." does it become a handicap.

When I gave this particular bit of wisdom to some of my students last year, a third grader immediately challenged me. "But, Mrs. Bru," she said, "you always say you can't draw or do sports."

"That's right," I agreed, "but maybe if I put my mind to it and really, really tried, I *could*. After all, it took me until the end of third grade to learn to read, but I finally managed to figure it out. Reading was much harder for me than drawing or sports, but I wanted to learn to read more than anything. Drawing and sports are things I really don't care much about so I never bothered to learn how. The only thing stopping me from drawing pictures or playing baseball is me."

Though my third graders were quite surprised that a *teacher* actually had trouble learning to read, I am by no means unique. Researchers followed a group of youngsters with L.D. all the way through school and into adulthood. In almost every case, the adults had managed to overcome their disability in one way or another. To anyone with experience in L.D., this doesn't come as much of a surprise. The amazing thing is that in over ninety percent of the cases the very thing that had been their disability as a child was now either their job or their hobby! Why? Because they'd worked so hard to 'beat' their difficulties, they felt a deep sense of satisfaction every time they proved to themselves they'd won.

Anna was unable to read as a child. Now she's a literary agent who reads for a living. Robert had a terrible time with math as a youngster. Today, he runs a small business and keeps his own books with little difficulty. My own particular disability is in the realm of written language and visual motor. I had an even harder time learning to write and spell than learning to read. Yet, I have half a dozen books, both fiction and nonfiction, in print.

Does this mean Anna, Robert and I are cured? Not even close. I can't speak for Anna or Robert, but I deal with my own learning disabilities every day of my life. I take an unbelievable amount of razzing for my handwriting, which sometimes even I can't read. I know three phone numbers, my social security number, and my zip code. Everything else I have to write down including the combination to my mailbox. I can't tell if my clothes match. Handicrafts and needlework are a study in frustration for me. I don't do anything even remotely athletic except exercises that take little or no coordination. Although I'm in fairly good shape, aerobics are an embarrassment. I don't know right from left without thinking about it. My short term memory is nonexistent, and if I write a note to myself, I lose it.

In spite of all that, people are shocked when I tell them I have a learning disability. Why? Because over the years I have built so many compensations for my difficulties that others aren't even aware of it. Every adult with L.D. that I know not only has dozens of compensation skills, each one seems to have a special gift that helps them overcome the worst of their learning disabilities.

Anna, for instance, says because she reads word by word, she picks up nuances of the language others miss. When I told my brother Rush that, he not only knew what she meant, he said he did exactly the same thing. As far as he's concerned, those of us who read whole paragraphs are missing the true beauty and cadence of the words. In fact, he says that's the reason writing poetry comes easily to him.

Michael is a truck driver with a reading disability who spends most of his time making deliveries in unfamiliar towns and cities. Though he can read, he does it too slowly to decipher street signs when he's driving. His salvation is a collection of detailed maps. He stops just before he enters the city, memorizes the map and then drives straight to his delivery point. Michael says he simply pictures the map in his head as he goes through the city. He's one of the few drivers from his company who rarely gets lost!

Had reading come easily for Anna, Rush or Michael, it's doubtful whether they would have developed their special 'gift'; they'd have had no need to. I could give you a hundred other examples to illustrate my point, but I think you get the idea. Once children with L.D. become aware of how they learn, they usually begin to compensate. They often catch up with their peers and sometimes even surpass them.

The hidden gifts and compensations may show up at any time in a child's life. Some kids 'click' while still in elementary school while others take longer. The important thing to remember is that the more support and understanding you give your child, the easier it will be for them to conquer their own L.D. monster.

Now that you have my personal explanation of learning disabilities, it's time to take a look at how the rest of the world views them. If you are reading this book, chances are you or someone close to you has been diagnosed as learning disabled or L.D. So what exactly is L.D.? The actual definition of L.D. varies from state to state, as do the regulations that determine whether a child qualifies for special education services. Your local school district or the State Department of Education can provide you with that information.

To be labeled L.D. in many states, a child must have an average or above IQ and show a severe discrepancy between ability and achievement. Translated, that means they have normal intelligence but are way behind their peers in reading, math, written language or oral expression.

Actually, L.D. is a bit more complicated than that. Not all students with L.D. fit the criteria, nor do the tests always show the true story. For one thing, a child will often function differently and score much higher in a quiet room with a single adult tester than in a noisy classroom. Another problem with testing happens when the learning disability hides a high IQ or a high IQ hides the learning disability.

Jonathan had problems from first grade on. By fifth grade, he was struggling in math to the point his parents and teacher felt a referral to special ed. was necessary. After the testing was finished, his parents and teacher met with the diagnostician and resource teacher who had done the testing. According to the intelligence test, Jonathan's IQ came out 80, which is 20 points below what is considered average and is in the "slow" range. His math scores were third grade level, which is consistent with the 80 IQ. He didn't qualify for special education because there was no discrepancy between his ability (IQ) and his achievement (third grade math.) In other words, the tests said he was doing the best he could be expected to.

Anyone who worked with Jonathan knew he wasn't a "slow learner". In fact, his reading was two years above grade level. Clearly, the test was not an accurate measure of Jonathan's intelligence. A learning disability was quite probably hiding his true IQ. Unfortunately, many students who truly do have L.D. slip through the cracks because the numbers on the tests don't fit the criteria. According to the law, if a student doesn't qualify within the criteria, that student can not receive services. If you feel your child is one of these, there are some options open to you which are discussed at length in chapter 14.

You may have heard terms like Dyslexia, Dyscalculia, and Dysgraphia used in reference to L.D. All three are names for different groups of learning disabilities. Generally, Dyslexia refers to problems with reading, spelling and understanding the written word. Dyscalculia involves difficulty with numbers and math concepts. Dysgraphia pertains to the physical act of writing and other visual motor tasks as well as problems with spelling and producing written language. All three may include long and short term memory problems and difficulty understanding oral directions as well as a variety of other hindrances to learning.

There are dozens of different labels for all types of learning disabilities. Unfortunately, people with L.D. don't fit into such neat little categories. Rarely will you find a person who has all the symptoms of one and none of the others. Every learning disability is as different and unique as the people who have them. Say you have two third graders with dyslexic type reading problems. One learns best through phonics and couldn't do flash cards if his life depended on it. The other can't sound words out worth spit, but really shines when presented with whole words. If you have five children who have trouble reading, chances are good they will have five different sets of problems.

Each child has his or her own strengths and weaknesses and has to be taught accordingly. For that reason, this book won't generally use terms like Dyslexia. Instead, it focuses on different areas of difficulty like reading or math. No child has every learning disability, and the same methods won't work for all. [1]

Once you accept *learns differently* as the definition of L.D., you begin to understand why your bright, creative child has difficulty in school. What may be obvious to teachers and other students isn't always that way for the child with a learning disability.

When I was doing my student teaching, I developed a unit on telling time. I taught the usual 'big hand' and 'little hand' concepts and everything seemed to be going well except for one little girl who absolutely couldn't get it. Beth's answers weren't just slightly off; they were so totally wrong they didn't

---

[1] Dyslexia is discussed briefly in Chapter 6. Also, if you're interested in Dyslexia and its relatives, there are many good books dealing with the subject. Check with your local library or your state Parent Training Center. (see Chapter 15 for a listing of PICs in your area)

even make sense. When the clock said 3:00, for instance, she'd read it as 6:15, and 8:15 would be 9:40. Nothing I did seemed to help. Finally, in utter frustration, Beth asked me, "Which little hand do you mean?"

Thinking she didn't know which was the minute hand and which was the hour hand, I used the terms long and short instead. "But which set of hands?" she wanted to know. As we went through it one more time, her friend suddenly spoke up.

"Oh, I get it," she said. "Beth's looking at the *other* little hands."

Now I was confused. "What other little hands?"

"You know the really little hands." It took several minutes and a pointer stick to make me understand what they were talking about. The hands on the classroom clock were attached to the face with a pin. About ½ an inch of each hand stuck out beyond the pin. It was those ½ inches that Beth thought I meant when I said the 'little hands'. I'd never even noticed them. Once Beth understood which 'hands' I was talking about, she had no further trouble.

Frequently, a student with L.D. will come up with his or her own 'way' of doing something. Quite often those methods don't make sense to teachers or parents. My husband is a classic example. He claims the only math teacher he ever learned from was the one who left him alone and let him work problems his own way. I never realized how different my husband's 'own way' of doing math was until I heard him explain multiplication by fives to our youngest son. I had always told Paul to count on his fingers by five, but he had difficulty remembering how to do that. My husband told him to divide the number in half and move the decimal point. (i.e. ½ of 6 is 3.0 so 5 X 6=30). It seemed convoluted and far more difficult to me, but it made sense to my son. Suddenly he could multiply by fives and get it right every time! I guarantee no teacher ever taught my husband that little trick. In fact, I'll bet he had to hide it so his teachers wouldn't make him do the work over the "right" way. If your child comes up with something that works, encourage them to use it instead of insisting they try a "simpler" way.

Sometimes your child may need academic crutches to get beyond a certain point in their learning. It may be the only way they can learn what they need to know. Take Trixie, for instance. Trixie came to me as a fourth grader. Because she didn't qualify for Special ed. early on, her parents had provided her with a math tutor. She could do addition and subtraction using touch points[2] including borrowing and carrying. It was clearly time to start her on multiplication. We went through the manipulative stage, and she gained a fair understanding of what multiplication was, then began memorizing her multiplication facts. That's when we hit a brick wall. No matter what method I used, she just couldn't seem to memorize those facts. By the end of the first quarter of fifth grade, she still didn't even know her 2's. I finally called it quits and gave her a multiplication table to use.

With the table we progressed on through double digit multiplication and division without too much trouble. She didn't know the facts but was able to grasp the concepts of what we were doing. Then we came to fractions. Given her difficulties learning the facts, I expected Trixie to have a tough time. I couldn't have been more wrong. For some reason she took to fractions like a duck to water. Even the most difficult fifth grade fraction problem was a snap for her. If I asked what is 3/4 of 12, she'd get a far off look in her eye, think for a minute and then say "nine".

Needless to say, I asked her how she did it. She said she just pictured a stack of 12 hay bales, split them into groups of four, then counted up three groups. Suddenly, I had a way to teach her multiplication facts. It took me a while to make her understand that what she was doing with fractions was actually multiplication, but gradually she began depending less and less on her multiplication table. By the time she hit 7th grade, she no longer needed it at all.

---

[2] See "TouchMath®" in Chapter 3, Math

If I hadn't given Trixie that multiplication table for a crutch, she might never have progressed beyond that point in math. When she no longer needed it, she threw it away.

A parent recently told me she thought it was wrong to give a child a crutch like that. Not only was it unfair to the other kids, the child might well become dependent on it. I told her it was much like she and I both wearing glasses. I only have to wear mine when I drive. She, on the other hand, is practically blind without hers. When I pointed out that she was completely dependent on her glasses and still managed to pull a 4.0 in college, she finally understood. How fair would it be for me to deny her the use of her glasses in a classroom just because I don't need mine?

So what if your child counts on his fingers or uses a spell checker? Plenty of adults do both. Personally, I never write anything that I want someone to be able to read without a computer. Denying your child the use of the tools he needs is only throwing unnecessary roadblocks in his way. Students with L.D. have enough problems to deal with without that.

As you progress through this book, you will find long lists of strategies to try with your child. Not all of them will be successful. Use them as starting points to help your child find his own way. As you and your child work through the process and experiment, you will very likely come up with your own strategies. Remember, no matter how thick your battering ram, some doors can not be broken through. Sometimes it's better to back off, rethink the method of attack, and then tunnel under the gate.

There is no cure for L.D., but the prognosis for your child is good. I can't promise they will become 'normal' or that they will always be successful. What I can promise is that your child has as good a chance for a happy successful life as any other.

Chapter 2
Reading
I could read,
But it would exceed,
The time I want to spend.
Louis R. Lampman (Adult with L.D.)

Reading. Most of us take it for granted. You do it a thousand times a day without a thought. Take a moment to reflect back over your day and think of all the times you read something. Chances are you used your reading skills a dozen different times before you even left the house for work: the toothpaste tube, the back of the cereal box, the note your daughter needed signed for school. Our world is run on the printed word. Even computers rely on it.

Now, imagine what it would be like if you suddenly couldn't read. In an instant, life becomes incredibly more difficult. Information of all sorts is inaccessible to you. You can't apply for a job, find your way across an unfamiliar town, or even figure out how to cook a frozen pizza. Everybody around you reads with effortless ease. What if they discover you can't? It becomes an embarrassing little secret that you tuck away and hope no one finds out.

I developed the following exercise to give you some sense of what it is like to have a reading disability. The first portion tells you how to do the activity. The letters *p d b q* are used interchangeably. If you look at them closely you will find that

L.D. From the Inside Out

they look exactly alike except for their orientation in space. Many students with L.D. can't tell the difference between them. A slight distortion has also been added to make the exercise a bit more challenging. Other than those slight modifications, the words and spacing have not been changed. Keeping that in mind, you should be able to decode the directions. Remember, this part will tell you how to do the rest, so read it out loud to make sure you understand.

The second part is the actual reading passage portion of this exercise. There are no distortions and no letter reversals. Admittedly, it is written in code, but it's a code you understand well and use every day. Phonics. Since every word in the following story follows some phonetic rule from the English language, you should have no trouble reading it, right?

Finally, you will be asked some questions. For an extra challenge, they are written phonetically *and* have the *p, b, d, q* reversals. Before you begin, better sharpen your pencil. You will need it if you are to follow the directions. Have phun!

[The following passage is rendered with scrambled spacing and letter positions to simulate a reading disability:]

Directions: This is a reading test. You'll be asked to read the first answer some questions. Reading the story aloud through the abilities and efore you answer the questions. Use your pencil to mark important bases. Sort our graph Pengos be n the qassages. If you ipently. Make sure you understand the pitions d or you qegin.

Wonce apon uh thyme Sleaping Buttey went two vizit thu three beirz. On hur weigh shee met thu beeg bad woolph. He was huphing, and puphing, and wheazing, and sneazing.

"Whut's rong?" Sleaping Buttey asct.

Thu woolph wyped his I's. "Alirjeez."

"Hear, tri a cuple of theas." Sleaping Buttey reecht inntoo hur bascit, puld owt a boughtul of Muthur Goose'z Shur-Feyer kure-ol pilsz and handid itt two thu wulph.

Thu wulph phround at thu botl hee helled inn hiz pa. "Whut r tha?"

"Sumthng eye got frum meye deer auld granee." Sleaping Buttey smeyeld and patid hyme awn thu hed. "Doan't wery, Sknow Wheyet yousd thm on won ov thu sevin dwoarfs. Hee had hae feevr soo bad thay yoused two cawl hymn Sneazee. Thoz pilz werct sew wel that hee wuz eighbol too chainj hiz naem two Rumplestiltskin.

Thu woolph thanct Sleaping Buttey and tha went thair seprute waz. Az phar az enywon nowz tha boath livd hapilee evr aftr.

   dueschuns
1. Whoo wus Sleaping Buttey going to see?
2. Frum the beetalez in the stoaree, wheye bo yoo subdoze shee wus going two sea them?
3. Whut else pue yoo thingc meigh hav qin in the dascit desipz the pillz? 4. Wheye po yoo thingk az you bo?
5. Whoo iz thu droatagunist ov thiss stoaree?
6. Naim the sevan bhairee teighlz this storee incoardoreights.
7. Is this stoaree phikshun?
8. Wood yoo klasipheye it as wreealitee or dhantusea? Wheye?
9. Lyst the dassidgez you unprlyneq and exdlayn wheye you thot tha wer imdortunt.

Wasn't that an entertaining little exercise? How well do you think you did? Did you have any difficulty underlining the important passages? Did you even know you were supposed to? Were you able to understand the directions and complete the questions or did you give up halfway through? Perhaps you took one look, decided it wasn't worth doing, and skipped the whole exercise. If you found yourself frustrated and confused, or refused to even start, this exercise was a success. Welcome to the world of L.D.

Reading is very complex brain function. In Kindergarten and first grade, teachers begin the long process of teaching children to decode the mysterious scribbles we call words. For any student it is much like climbing a steep mountain path. It is very difficult, and it will be years before they are completely proficient at it. For a child with a learning disability, it's more like struggling though the foothills pulling a fully loaded wagon while your classmates are dashing up the trail ahead with nothing to hold them back.

My students are usually the children for whom reading is an unfathomable mystery. Even so, I have never met a child who didn't *want* to learn how to read. Many are so beat up by the system that they no longer want to try, but that burning desire is still there deep down inside. The truly remarkable thing is that many of them do keep trying day after day, year after year. For many it becomes a constant struggle to prove to themselves and the world that they aren't stupid.

If you think I made your reading task unnecessarily hard, think again. Reading truly is this difficult for some children. Several years ago one of our second grade teachers did a simple reading test to determine at what level each child was reading comfortably. Few of the students had any problem with the task. In fact, everything went fine until she came to Logan. He looked at the page for several seconds then pushed it back across the table to her. "I can't read this one," he said. "Do you have one in English?"

Imagine how frustrating it would be if all your school work were as difficult as my little reading exercise or if you were like Logan and didn't even recognize your native language. How long would it be before you gave up and refused to even try? Go back and read any part of the exercise out loud. You'll probably find you have to stop frequently to figure out a word. If you listen to yourself read, you'll realize you're making the same halting progress as many non-proficient readers.

Chances are when you did the exercise, you were a little uncertain of what exactly the directions were, at least the first time through. This is what a child with a reading disability lives with every day. To them, all words are written in code. The little squiggles we call the letters of the alphabet in reality have no meaning by themselves. There is nothing to give a hint at the sounds they stand for unless you understand the code.

Years ago, at the beginning of my career, I thought phonics was the only way to teach reading. I faithfully taught everything in the correct order, first consonant sounds, then long and short vowels, and blends. For my more advanced students it was diphthongs and diagraphs. I was secure in the knowledge that I was doing a good job of training my students in phonics and therefore teaching them to be good readers. And yet, there were always those who couldn't tell the difference between a short *i* sound and a short *e*.

It clearly didn't work for everyone, but at that point in time, I didn't know there was any other way to teach reading. Several years later, whole language came along. Unfortunately, it didn't work any better than phonics. There were still children who didn't learn to read, not the same ones perhaps, but more than enough to fill my class.

Over the years, I've seen many philosophies come and go. Our district has tried everything from direct instruction and phonics to whole language and total immersion. One thing has become abundantly clear. There are *no* silver bullets. Every program has its own strengths and weaknesses, but no program on earth will work for every child. Yet, I truly believe there *is* a magic combination for every child that unlocks the mystery of reading. The trick is finding it.

I often find myself using a technique very different from the method currently embraced by my district. Only children who are having difficulty learning in the regular classroom are in my class. It makes little sense to continue teaching with the same technique that has already failed them. From each new philosophy, I've added something to my bag of tricks. If a literacy-based program doesn't seem to work, for instance, I pull out phonics. A child who flounders with phonics may be more successful using a sight word program. I often combine several different programs until I find the combination that works for that particular child.

Remember Logan, the child who didn't recognize English? At the time he was placed in the resource room, our district was using an Early literacy approach to reading. The emphasis was on comprehension; children were expected to use meaning to figure out unfamiliar words. This method was very successful for many students but not Logan. It was obvious he needed something different.

I put him in a program called Visual phonics which uses a unique set of symbols and hand signs to represent all the phonetic sounds. At the same time I started teaching him to recognize sight words. It worked. By using phonics to sound out the words he couldn't get from context clues, reading suddenly began to make sense to him. As his decoding skills improved so did his reading. By the beginning of third grade he was starting to catch up and by the end of the first semester it was time to get him ready to go back into the regular classroom.

At first we eased into the third grade book, but as he gained confidence, we began to move faster. At the beginning of the final quarter, Logan rejoined his class for reading. Though I monitored his progress for the rest of third grade and all of fourth, Logan never again floundered with his reading. When his re-evaluation came up in fifth grade, Logan tested out at nearly a year above grade level in reading.

Finding what works for each child is the tough part. I could tell you stories much like Logan's where a phonetic approach was the villain, and Early literacy the knight in shining armor. Just as there are no silver bullets, the right combination is different for each child. Don't give up right away because something doesn't seem to work. No matter what you use, it will take time for your child to learn enough for it to show in their reading. On the other had, don't make the mistake many teachers do and stick with a program that obviously isn't working.

Below are explanations of three of the most common approaches to reading.

PHONICS/ SOUND SYMBOL

A phonetic approach is based on word attack skills, or the deciphering of unknown words using rules of phonics. According to *Webster's Ninth Collegiate Dictionary*, phonics is the representation of speech sounds by means of symbols. In our language those symbols are the alphabet in various combinations. These combinations are called phonemes and are the basis of our written language. In the phonetic approach, children are taught letter sounds and phonetic rules before attempting words. While all this is going on, the teacher is reading to them, sharing books, pointing out relationships in rhyming words, and letting them practice their phonetic skills. Then, when they are ready, they move into simple books.

The problem is that there are many, many phonetic rules and none of them are always true. Take for instance the words c*a*ke, c*a*t, *a*bout, *a*wful, *a*ir, and c*a*rt. The letter *a* has a different sound in each word. To complicate matters you have words like ate and eight. We know the *a* in ate is a long *a* because of the silent *e* on the end. But why in heaven's name does eigh also sound like a long *a*?

One day, back at the beginning of my career when I taught only phonics, I happened by the lunch line just as the fifth graders were going in. One of my students called me over. "Hey, Mrs. Bru, I just said 'the big F word' to the principal." For those of you who may not have heard the term, 'the big F word' is exactly what it sounds like, the biggest, baddest, most terrible four letter curse word in the English language, or at least it was then. Back in the seventies, saying that word would have landed any kid in hot water up to his neck. Since Doug was still standing in line and not cooling his heels in the office, I was pretty sure he hadn't said it to Mr. Durr.

"Really," I said, deciding to play it cool.

Doug flashed me a big grin. "Yup, I said the biggest 'F' word I know, Philadelphia!"

I had a really tough time convincing him there wasn't a single 'F' in the word Philadelphia. The very next day I started teaching him sight words.

EARLY LITERACY/ WHOLE LANGUAGE

An Early literacy approach is almost the complete opposite of a phonics program. Early literacy and whole language programs work on the principal of immersion and are based on comprehension, or reading for understanding. The child is surrounded by the printed word. Words cover the walls of the classroom. Every available table sports a literacy center or two. Students write as a group, figuring out words as they go, and they read constantly. Unlike a phonetic approach, children begin the process of learning to read by reading. They start with simple, predictable books and progress through levels as they are ready for them. They rely heavily on pictures and context clues.

The problem with the Early literacy approach is that children aren't given many strategies to decipher words they don't know. If they can't figure out a word from the picture or the context of the sentence, they don't know how to 'sound' it out. Recently I had a student who simply was not progressing through the program. After two and a half years Julie was still reading at an early Kindergarten level. It was nearly impossible for her to figure out words from the context.

Normally I would not have waited so long to try something different, but our district was involved in a 'new' program and we, as teachers, were being watched rather closely to make sure we were 'teaching correctly'. I had exhausted all the methods we had been taught and still Julie wasn't getting it.

When I explained the problem to my 'reading mentor', she gave me the only other method in the program I hadn't tried. When Julie came to a word she didn't know, she was to make a list of all the words that could make sense in the sentence and figure out which it was. This would be an extremely cumbersome way for an adult to figure out an unfamiliar word. For Julie it was a completely unusable strategy. I went against our 'reading program' and taught her phonics. She progressed rapidly after that.

SIGHT WORDS

If Phonics and Early literacy are on opposite ends of the spectrum, sight word programs are somewhere in the middle. Sight words are words that a reader knows by sight and doesn't have to figure out. Eventually all words become sight words no matter what reading program you are using. There are some, however, like *want* and *only*, that are always classified as sight words because the only way to learn them is to memorize them.

In a sight word program, students learn whole words rather than learning the phonetic pieces. They start with words like *the, and, I*, then progress to more difficult words. Like phonics, students who learn sight words have a pretty solid basis before they actually begin reading books. Even in the upper levels, there is a vocabulary lesson before every story where the words from the story are taught and explained. Sight word programs depend heavily on context clues though not as much as the Early literacy programs do.

Like a literacy program, sight word programs depend on word recognition and don't teach word-attack skills. Because the words are introduced in isolation, it is more difficult for children to attach meaning to them than with Early literacy programs. Words like *read* and *wind* become very confusing. They are pronounced differently depending on how they are used in the sentence. For instance *read* in the sentence *'I have **read** that story six times,'* sounds different than in *"Did you **read** that book?"* That's bad enough, but at least they both mean basically the same thing. Now take a look at *wind*. Is it *wind* like *"The **wind** is blowing."* or like, *"Don't forget to **wind** your watch."* There is no way to know unless it is used in context.

Though I may well be a minority, I believe a good solid base in all three methods will give your child the greatest chance of mastering reading in and out of school. Since I use phonics, Early literacy, and sight words all at the same time, the lines between them tend to blur. In a nut shell, the knowledge of phonics gives children word-attack skills. It provides them with the tools they need to sound out unfamiliar words. Early literacy technique helps children to gain meaning from what they read and teaches the use of context clues. Learning sight words helps students with words that are neither phonetic nor necessarily make sense in context.

What can you as a parent do to help your child become a good reader? It has been said that there are five ways to improve reading skills. Read, read, read, read, and read. It isn't far from the truth. The best thing you can possibly do for your child's reading is to set aside at least twenty minutes every evening to read to and with your child. I have never met a child who didn't like to be read to. Getting kids to *like* reading books is half the battle. Below are some strategies to teach reading as well as some suggestions to help develop a love for reading. Don't be afraid to mix and match.

* When working with beginning readers have them point to each word as they read.
* When you are reading with your child don't tell them words they are having difficulty with. Encourage them to use word-attack and context clue strategies to figure out unfamiliar words.
* Teach your child how to use context and picture clues to figure out unknown words:
* Skip the word and read to the end of the sentence. What word would make sense?
* Reread.
* Look at the picture for clues.
* Think of what is going on in the story. What word would make sense?
* Teach them to use word attack skills:
* Sound it out
* What sound does it start with?
* Stretch the word out (c-a-t)

* Are there any chunks of the word you know? (fly-**ing**)
* Are there any 'little' words that you know? (c-**and**-y)
* If they still can't figure out a word, tell them what it is.
* Encourage your child to read for meaning by asking them questions and discussing what they are reading.
* Teach sight words (flash cards are available at many discount and department stores, or you can make your own on index cards.) Start small with one or two words then expand slowly as your child conquers more and more words.
* For young children, buy a set of magnetic letters for the outside the refrigerator. Make a game of forming words and encourage them to do the same. As they progress, begin making simple sentences
* For older, more advanced readers, words with magnetic backing can be purchased from many bookstores or school supply stores. A cookie sheet, file cabinet, or refrigerator work well for work areas. Begin with a few simple words. Challenge various family members to create phrases and sentences. Turn it into a game. Don't try this until your child has mastered enough words to make it fun.
* School supply stores carry a variety of materials for teaching phonics from workbooks to games. Many of these can also be purchased in discount stores in the coloring book and toy sections.
* If you wish to try a full blown phonics program, there are many available. You've no doubt seen some advertised on T.V. If you choose to use one of them, be aware that many commercial phonics programs move too rapidly for most students with L.D. You may have to expand and adapt the program for your child. If it seems to be moving too quickly, do the activities for longer periods or create similar activities that do the same thing.
* Visual Phonics- This program is one I have used with great success over the years. It uses visual, auditory *and* tactile input. Though it is not a silver bullet, it's as close as I have ever seen. I have found very few individuals it did not work

for. It even seems to improve spelling skills though I can't say that I ever figured out why.[3]

* Pick books that appeal to your child, in fact have them help you pick.

* Read interesting or amusing books to your child. Nothing grabs a child faster than an entertaining story. Don't worry if they want to hear/read the same one over and over. Over-learning is a very effective learning strategy. Share the reading with your child. I usually follow the rule of 2- 1. Depending on the book and the reading level of the child, I read two paragraphs, or pages to their one.

* Don't worry if they choose books that are somewhat above their reading level if it is a topic that interests them. Harry Potter has taught more than one of my students to read. Be prepared to help with the tough words, though.

* By the same token, it's ok to read books you think are too simple as long as your child doesn't view the book as babyish. Nothing gives a child confidence like being able to do something easily. You want to foster the perception that reading can be easy and fun.

* Discuss the book as you read it. "What do you think is going to happen? Why did he/she do that? Wow, I wasn't expecting that!" etc. Do this for books you read to them as well as the books you read together.

* Have casual conversations about the books you are reading with your child at times other than when you are reading them. "Who do you think the bad guy is? Or "I think Henry is up to no good. What do you think?" etc.

* Read books from which some of their favorite movies have been made. Discuss similarities and differences.

* Vary the reading level of the books you read together. Make sure there is a good mixture of books that are easy, ones that are difficult, and be sure that the biggest share of them are

---

[3] For more information on Visual Phonics visit the website www.icli.org.

at a comfortable reading level. The number one deciding point should be that your child *wants* to read it.

* If possible, take your book with you and read during down time, like when you're waiting at the doctor's or dentist's office. You can also have your child read to you on the way home from the sitter or on the way to the grocery store. Not only will it encourage reading, it will make time pass faster.

* Let your child see you read for pleasure as well as other types of reading you might do. Believe it or not, statistics show the number one determiner of whether a child will become a reader is if the child sees his or her parents reading, especially the father.

If a child with a reading disability is beyond the third grade, teaching that child to read isn't enough. During the first three years of school the emphasis is on *learning to read*. About fourth grade, the emphasis becomes *reading to learn*. By upper elementary, students are asked to get information by reading a variety of sources including text books, encyclopedias, and dictionaries. For a child with a reading disability, this adds another layer of frustration. They may understand what is going on in science and social studies but can't read the materials and consequently are unable to complete assignments.

Frances and Isabel were both fifth graders with reading problems. Frances could read almost anything at grade level but didn't understand one word of what she'd read. Isabel, on the other hand, had great comprehension but could only decode at about a first grade level. Though they came to my class at the same time, it would have been ludicrous to put them in the same reading program; their needs were completely different.

I put Isabel in a strong phonics curriculum that taught decoding skills and began an intensive sight word program with her. At the same time, I immersed Frances in novels. By using context clues, paying attention to picture cues, and making predictions, we dissected stories, searching for meaning. Both girls began to progress and their skills improved.

Though Frances and Isabel were making good progress in their reading, they still had the 5th grade curriculum to contend with, and neither had the reading skills required. The solution was simple: Frances read the material out loud, Isobel interpreted, and they both did their own work. By teaming them, each was given a way around their disability.

Of course, this particular solution was a fluke. I've had other students like Frances and Isabel but never at the same time. Even so, the solutions to difficulties caused by learning disabilities frequently lay within the child themselves. There is often a strength or a talent that can be used to off-set the disability.

Isobel had a phenomenal auditory memory. If she heard it, she remembered it. It would have been a simple matter to read her text books to her or put her into the books on tape program. Most students with learning disabilities qualify for a program called *recordings for the visually impaired*, better known as Books on Tape[4]. It was created for blind or visually impaired students but is available for children with learning disabilities as well. Through this program, a student is provided with an audio copy of the textbooks from appropriate classes and a tape player. Isabel's reading disability wouldn't interfere as she would be able to gather the information she needed through her ears.

Books on Tape probably wouldn't have done Frances any good since her difficulty was comprehension, not decoding. She needed important points identified and explained. In her case, I would have gone over every chapter in her textbooks, identifying and explaining important concepts. Below are some strategies that help students focus on important details in

---

[4] States differ in what agency handles *recordings for the visually impaired*. Contact your local school district or your department of education to find about more about this service in your area. If your child is labeled L.D. they probably qualify for this service.

content reading. Even students who don't have comprehension problems find these strategies useful.

1. Read all questions in your assignment before beginning to read the chapter. That way you will know what information to look for.

2. Focus on subtopics in the chapter. Most textbooks are divided into sections. The most important idea or fact is often presented at the beginning of the section in boldfaced or italicized letters.

3. Pay attention to boldfaced or italicized words within the text. They usually indicate important concepts.

4. Read all picture captions.

5. Highlight important text. Many middle school and high school resource rooms have highlighted copies of the textbooks available. If yours does not, most office supply stores have removable highlighter tape. You can stick it right on the page over important passages then remove it when it is no longer needed.

6. Jot down notes to remember important details. Don't make them too involved. A word or two is usually enough.

Remember the core of any reading program is read, read, read. Surround your children with books that they enjoy. Read to them and with them often. If they **don't** already have a library card, get them one. Take them to the library as often as you can and get them involved in the library reading programs.

There is another facet of a reading disability that needs mention here. Many reading difficulties, particularly those associated with Dyslexia, are caused by perceptual and/or processing problems. This topic is discussed further in Chapter 6.

Chapter 3
Math

The confusion of Math
Blocked my path,
And me with no place
to cut and run!
Louis R. Lampman

On the surface, math might appear less difficult to learn than reading. After all, there are only a handful of symbols, and we can use manipulatives to *see* the concepts. Unfortunately, to a child with a math learning disability it means learning a whole new set of rules, many of which are in conflict with each other and with rules they've already learned.

Up until this point everything the child does starts at the left of the page and moves to the right. On a math worksheet, the problems start on the left and move across the page to the right just like reading. However, when a student starts to work the problem the rules change. Now they are to begin with the number on the right ('ones') and work to the left. That's only one of the many rules that make math confusing.

To give you a feel for what it's like to have a math disability, I have created a new numeration system. The rules are the same as you have always used. Only the symbols and the names of some of the operations have changed. To really "get it" you need to actually work the problems. If you'd rather not do this exercise, so much the better. Kids with a math disability aren't given the option of not doing their work. So pick up a pencil and give it your best shot.

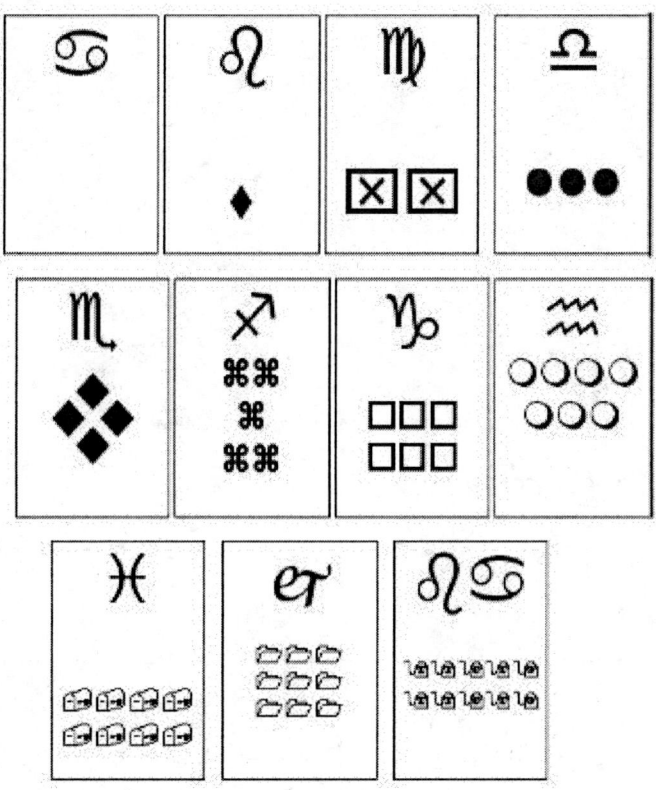

L.D. From the Inside Out

The number line below will give you a feel for the new number system. Feel free to refer to it as you are working the problems on the next few pages.

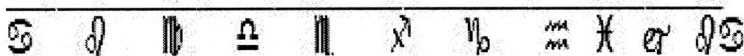

Here are some Kindergarten and first grade problems for you to try.

Circle the correct numeral	
• • • • • ♎ ♏ ♐	🐦🐦🐦🐦 🐦🐦🐦🐦 ♓ ♈ ♏
🐚🐚🐚🐚🐚🐚🐚 🐚🐚🐚🐚🐚🐚 ♌♌ ♎♌ ♌♎	○○○○○ ○○ ○○○○○ ♌♍ ♍♌ ♌♌

Write the correct numeral ♓♓♓♓ ♓♓♓ _____	♈♈♈♈♈♈♈♈♈ ♈♈♈♈♈♈♈♈♈ _____
Draw a set to match the numeral ♍	♏
♌♌	♌♑

Since you now know all the numerals, let's try some operations. First we'll start with ebbition. Ebbing is combining numbers. When you see the _ sign it means to ebb. For instance b _ d = e

Dabtraction is the opposite of ebbition. It means to take away. ^ is the sign for dabbtracting. So e ^ d = b. Simple isn't it? All right, here are a few problems for you to try. Remember to watch your signs!

♌ _ ♌ _ ♎ _ ♌♍ _ ♍♑ _ ♍ _ ♑ _ ♍♎
♐♌ ♐♍ ♐♎ ♐♌♍ ♈♌ ♈♐ ♈♍

Now let's try some more difficult ebbition and dabtraction. Remember, you may have to borrow and carry.

[astrological symbol math problems]

Since you have now mastered ebbition and dabtraction, it's time to move on to lumtoplacation and vidision. Lumtoplaing is just ebbing the same number over and over again. Vidision is the opposite. For instance c ＿ c ＿ c ＿ c =i so c x e =i and i y c =e . The best way to learn lum-toplacation and vidision is to memorize the facts. Here are the c s.

[astrological symbol multiplication and division tables]

That brings us to the middle of third grade. I doubt if many of you are still trying to work the "math" problems. For those of you who are, just think, the next step is double digit lumtoplacation and long vidision. If that doesn't send you screaming from the room, there are always fractions and decimals, not to mention time, money, measurement, and everyone's all time favorite, story problems.

The symbols used in this exercise were specially chosen. Not only are most of them difficult to write, several of them look similar to each other. The symbols we have come to recognize as numbers are no less foreign. The only reason we know what they mean is that we have learned to associate each with a specific amount.

How did it feel to work problems when you still didn't have a solid concept of the amount each numeral stood for? When you got frustrated you probably quit, just as a child does. The difference was you didn't have anyone standing over your shoulder forcing you to get back to work and telling you how easy it is if you'd just pay attention.

As you can see, math is more difficult than it first appears. Were c and e confusing? In reality they look less alike than 6 and 9. How about b c and c b ? We assume that children will automatically see the difference between 12 and 21. Think about how similar they look and how different the amounts they stand for are. Not only that, numerals have different names when they are in different positions. Take 3, 13, and 31 for instance. If that isn't confusing enough for you throw in a few zeros. 200 is two hundred, but 20010 is *not* two hundred ten, 210 is even though 21 is twenty-one. ARGH!

As you can see, math is more difficult than it first appears. Were E and F confusing? In reality they look less alike than 6 and 9. How about BC and CB? We assume that children will automatically see the difference between 12 and 21. Think about how similar they look and how different the amounts they stand for are. Not only that, numerals have different names when they are in different positions. Take 3, 13, and 31 for instance. If that isn't confusing enough for you throw in a few zeros. 200 is two hundred, but 20010 is not two hundred ten, 210 is even though 21 is twenty-one. ARGH!

There are all kinds of strange little quirks that we expect kids to pick up. Even the things we say to help can add to the confusion. Imagine you are helping your third grader with subtraction. She hasn't quite grasped the concept of when to borrow and when not to. "You have to borrow if the bottom number is bigger," you say and point to her problem. "Now is 7 bigger than 2?"

She thinks about what you said, looks at the numbers, and wonders if you've lost your mind. Any fool can see that both numbers are the same size! In math we sometimes use the words bigger and smaller to mean amount, and sometimes to mean size. We expect children to know which meaning we are using.

There are many such conflicts in the language of math. If the problem says Suzy has three birds and David gives her two *more,* you add. But if the problem says Suzy has three birds and David has two; how many *more* does Suzy have, you are supposed to subtract.

Nor is it just the language that's difficult. If I add 16 and 23, it doesn't matter which number I put on top. The same is true of multiplication. Since we teach addition first, the child learns that placement of the numbers in the problem doesn't make any difference. Then we move on to subtraction. Suddenly it makes a great deal of difference; the biggest number always goes on top. Which brings us back to size. Is it any wonder a child with L.D. gets thoroughly bewildered?

If the exercise left you feeling confused and frustrated, you've had a small taste of what your child experiences every day. Think what it would be like to go through it again day after day, week after week. I venture to guess it wouldn't be long before you hated math. Most kids who hate math dislike it because they have trouble with it. The key is to make it easier for them, to explain it in a way that makes sense to them and to give them strategies for solving problems.

As you worked through the exercises, did you find yourself referring to the aids at the beginning? Chances are you did, and as you began to 'learn' the symbols you referred to them less and less. That is generally what happens with children and math aids. One of the most destructive things I've seen parents and teachers do is tell children they can't use crutches that help them learn math because they might become dependent on them. In reality, if you don't give kids math aids they need, they will often find their own. I've seen students use clocks, calendars, even the bricks on the walls to figure math problems. Why not provide them with reliable methods that work time after time?

Over the years I've learned not to fret about students becoming overly dependent on math aids. It is much like a child with a broken leg using crutches to get around. At first they love the novelty of it, but it soon becomes too cumbersome and slow for most kids. As soon as they can walk without aid, the crutches are discarded. Once students memorize facts and figure out how to work problems, they gradually move away from using the crutch.

The student who continues to count on his fingers or use touch points is probably one who needs to. So what? As long as it's a crutch they'll always have access to, there really isn't a problem. I teach kids to count on their fingers rather than to use a number line even though both work equally well in the beginning stages. Student will always have their fingers. Number lines are few and far between in the real world.

Students with L.D. have a tendency to find their own creative ways to do math. One of the best strategies I ever saw for teaching carrying came from a 4th grade student of mine. Dwayne seemed to grasp the concept of double digit multiplication but got the wrong answer about half the time. While watching him work through several problems, I realized he wasn't sure which digit to carry. Sometimes he carried the tens and got the correct answer; the rest of the time he carried the ones and didn't have a clue why he was wrong. I pointed out where he was making his mistake and went to help another student.

Several minutes later he called me back with a big grin on his face. "I figured it out!" he said. "All I have to do is write the number the way I say it." He demonstrated with the problem 45X7. "See, seven times five is 35 so I write the 3 over the 4 when I say 'thirty' and 5 in the ones place when I say 'five'."

```
  3
 45
 x7
  5
```

I'm pretty sure my mouth fell open. It was such an incredibly easy solution that I felt sort of silly not coming up with it myself. I've taught Dwayne's method to dozens of youngsters who were having the same problem. Invariably the light comes on the second they see it.

The following are other strategies to try. What works for one student won't necessarily work for another so don't be afraid to discard one and try something else. Be inventive. Find out what makes sense to your child and go from there. Many of these are methods students or I have come up with over the years and may work for your child as well.

Counting/ Numeral recognition:

1. *Counting games-* Have them count the items you buy in the grocery store (How many apples is that?) or things they see in their environment (How many dogs are there in that yard?) Make it a game.
2. *Matching games-* numerals to number of objects
3. *Follow the dots-* start with simple ones and gradually increase the difficulty.
4. *Finding numbers in the real world-* Have them read numbers to you from the clock, a calendar, speed limit signs, etc.
5. *Card games-* Go Fish, Concentration, Spoons, etc.
6. *Games with Spinners to indicate number of spaces moved.*

Addition:

1. *Using manipulatives-* Provide them with objects they can count; beans or buttons work very well. In the beginning stages you may have to have a different color or size for each of the two numbers they add.
2. *Counting on fingers-* In the beginning stages they use their fingers for both numbers they add. Once they reach ten, teach

them to put one number in their head and the other on their fingers then start counting. (9+5. The child puts up 5 fingers then touches the 9 with her other hand and begins counting on their fingers, *10, 11,12,13,14"*)

3. *Math strategies-* There are a whole series of math strategies for learning addition, subtraction, multiplication, and division facts. (Multiplying by two, for instance, is the same as adding doubles). If the only method your child knows for finding the answer is by counting on their fingers that is all they'll do. A really good source for these strategies is "Thinking Strategies For Mastering Math" [5] These materials are also great for students who 'get' concepts but have difficulty memorizing facts.

4. *TouchMath®-* This is a program created to help kids learn the operations. Each numeral has a series of touch points that equal its value. Students learn the position of the points and simply count them up to get the answer. Lower grade elementary teachers often have this program so you may want to ask around. If you can't find it, materials are available through Innovative Leaning Concepts.[6]

5. *Number lines-* Though I find the other three methods more useable, some students respond well to number lines, particularly in the beginning. Start with one of the numbers you are adding and move "up" (to the right) the number line the number of spaces indicated by the "smaller number". The number you land on will be the answer.

6. *Magic 9's for addition-* Whenever a number is added to 9 the answer ends in a numeral one less than the one added. So 9+**7**= 1**6** and 9+**3**= 1**2**

7. *Addition Bingo-* Just like regular Bingo except the cards contain addition problems and the "caller" calls out single numbers. Players cover problems that equal the number.

8. *Dominoes, triominoes, etc.*

---

[5] :Thinking Strategies for Mastering Math: www.masteringmath.com
[6] See Appendix 1 (resources)

9. *Dice Addition-* Each player gets a pair of dice (or can share one set) Each tosses the dice and add the faces. The one with the highest number wins the round. Keep tallies for number of rounds won.
10. *Board games that use two dice*
11. *Flash cards*

Subtraction

1. *Using manipulatives-* Provide them with objects they can count- beans or buttons work very well. Count out the "larger" number then take the smaller number away. This will help them understand the concept of why the "largest" has to go on top in a problem.
2. *Counting on their fingers-* Up to ten is the same as using manipulatives. After ten, however, there are two methods. *(A)Counting backward-* Put up the "smaller" number of fingers, then say the larger number and start counting backwards on your fingers. (11-4 would sound like "11,10, 9,8,7) 7 is the answer. *(B)Counting forward-* Put the "smaller" number in your head, then using your fingers count up to the "larger" one. Finally count the number of fingers you used to get the answer (11-4 would sound like "5,6,7,8,9,11.") You used 7 fingers so the answer is 7.
3. *A magic nine for subtraction.* In the problem 16-9, for instance, add the top two numbers together to get the answer. 1+6 = 7 so 16-9+7
4. *Math Stratigies-* See explanation under addition.
5. *TouchMath®-* -See explanation under addition.
6. *Number lines-* Start with the numeral with the highest value and move "down" (to the left) the number line the number of spaces indicated by the "smaller number." The number you land on will be your answer.
7. *Flash cards*

Place value

1. *Using manipulative-* Make numbers using base ten blocks and place value charts. Homemade bean sticks and place value

charts work as well.[7] For example, to make 64--- place 6 tens in the "tens place" on the place value chart and 4 ones in the "ones place". 46 would be 4 tens and 6 ones.

2. *Counting-* Give them groups of objects, beans, sequins, popcorn kernels, nails etc. And have them divide them into groups of ten on place value charts then write the number. The technique shows and easy way to count larger numbers as well as teaching the concept of place value.

3. *Dice Game 1-* Players will need dice of three different colors, a paper to write on and tokens of some kind. Designate which color is hundreds, which is tens and which is ones. Players take turns tossing the dice and writing and reading the numbers. For example if the hundreds dice was 3, the tens dice 6, and the ones dice 1, the number would be 361. If a player writes and reads the number correctly they earn a token. The player with the most tokens wins the game. This game can be played using 2, 3, or 4 dice.

4. *Dice game 2-largest number -* Players need two dice, a piece of paper and pencil and some sort of token. (I use Popsicle sticks) During their turn they throw the dice and write the largest number they can make with the two numbers. The next player does the same and so on until all players have written their numbers. Then they compare numbers and whoever has the largest number in each round takes a token. At the end of the game the player with the most tokens wins. The game can also be played for the smallest number. It can also be modified for hundreds and thousands by using three or four dice instead of two.

Regrouping (Borrowing and Carrying)
RULE to teach: No more than 9 can live in one column. A ten must move to the next column.

1. *Using manipulatives to carry-* Set problems up using base ten blocks or bean sticks and place value charts. For instance, for the problem 23+19. Set out two tens and 3 ones. Then add 1

---

[7] see section on homemade manipulatives

ten and 9 ones which gives you 3 tens and 12 ones. The rule is only 9 in a column so you trade 10 of the beans for a ten and leave 2 in the ones place. The final answer is 4 tens and 2 ones or 42.

2. *Using manipulatives to borrow*- Set problems up using base ten blocks or bean sticks and place value charts. For instance for the problem 23-19. Set out two tens and 3 ones then try to subtract 19. Since there are only 3 beans in the ones place you must go to the tens place and "borrow" a bean stick. You can't put a 10 in the ones column so you have to trade it in for 10 single beans which gives you 13 in the one's place and 1 in the tens place. Now you subtract. The answer is 12.

3. *Chip trading game*- Players will need base ten blocks (or bean sticks and single beans described in the manipulative section) place value charts, dice, pencil, & paper. Players throw one die and set up the number on their place value chart. On their next turn they throw the die again and add that number. If the resulting number is 10 or more, they must trade for a "ten" and place it in the TENS place. The first player to reach 100 is the winner. To play using subtraction, each player starts with 100 and subtracts with each toss of the dice. If there are not enough in the ONES column to subtract, they must "Borrow" a ten and break it into ones. (Players write the problems on paper to get used to the paper/pencil mechanics of regrouping.)

4. *Dimes and pennies*- If your child has a good solid concept of the value of money you can use dimes and pennies instead of bean sticks or base ten blocks. Dimes are tens and pennies are ones. Dollars can be used for 100's if you get that far. You can take it into real life by giving them pennies for something, every time they remember to hang up their coat for instance, which they can trade in for dimes, and then dollars. They can also lose a penny for each time they don't hang it up. If they don't have any pennies, then they have to trade in a dime for 10 pennies.

Multiplication- <u>**RULE to teach multi-plication is adding the same number over and over again.**</u>

1. *Using manipulative-* Manipulatives for multiplication may be any small objects that can be easily grouped. Snap beads or small building blocks that snap together work especially well. The problem 3x4 literally means 3 groups of 4. To work the problem, make three groups with four object each then count the objects.

You can also use an empty egg carton or 3x5 cards to get the concept of multiplication across. For the problem 3 times 4, have your child place 3 small objects, such as beans, onto 4 cards. Then count the total number of beans.

2. *Memorize facts-* For most students, memorization of facts is by far the easiest way to work multiplication problems especially when dealing with two and three digit problems. Even if the students can't remember all facts, they should be encouraged to memorize all they can.

3. *Tricks-* For students who have difficulty memorizing, there are "tricks" for figuring out multiplication problems.

A. *Counting by 2's, 5's etc.* - For twos put up the number of fingers you are multiplying by and count by 2. (For instance 2X5, put up five fingers and count 2, 4, 6, 8, 10). Five's work the same way except for counting by 5. (For 5X2, put up two fingers and count 5,10) It works for all numbers but 2's, 5's and 10's are easiest since most students can count by 2', 5's and 10's.

B. *Repetitive addition-* Since multiplication is actually adding the same number over and over again this can be used to solve multiplication problems. Say for instance you remember 3X5= 15 but can't remember 3X6. Simply start with 15 and count 3 more. 3X7 would be 3X5 then count three more, then three more again.

C. *1's & 0's.* These are fairly obvious but may need to be taught to some children. Anything X 0 = 0, and anything X 1= itself.

D. *2's-* Doubles. In other words 3+3=6 so 2X3=6; 8+8=16 so 2X8 =16 etc.

E. *4's-* Doubling doubles- 3X4 is the same as (3+3) and (3+3) added together. So 3+3=6 and 6+6=12.

F. *Eights* Once the child understands the concept of doubling doubles, eights can be taught using the same method.

G. *6's-* Any even number multiplied by 6 will give an answer ending in that number- **4X6= 24** and **8X6 =48**.

H. *Magic 9's for multiplication-* There are two tricks for magic 9's.

1. Place both hands in front of you on the table. Imagine they are numbered 1-10 starting with the little finger of your left hand and ending with the little finger of your right hand. Bend down the finger corresponding to the number you are multiplying by 9 (For 4X9 you'd bend your left pointer) Count everything to the left of the bent finger you count by 10, and everything to the right by ones. (4X9 would sound like: 10, 20, 30, 31, 32, 33, 34, 35, 36).

2. When added together, the numerals in the answer to any 9's multiplication problem will equal 9. The tens in any 9's multiplication problem is one less than the number you are multiplying. So if you want to multiply 9X6, your tens will be five (one less than 6) and the ones will be 4 (because 5+4=9) or 54.

I. *10's, 100's, 1000's etc.-* To multiply by 10 simply put a zero after the number you are multiplying. So 6X10=60 and 54X10=540. When multiplying by 100, you use two zeroes, for thousands you use three zeroes and so on.

J. *11's-* For the numbers 1-9 you write the number you are multiplying by twice. So 11X5=55 and 11X3=33.

4. *Using a multiplication table-* There are several uses for a multiplication table. If the class moves on to more difficult multiplication before your child has the facts memorized, a table will enable them to keep up. A table is also useful to look up facts that they can't memorize. I've had students who were unable to memorize anything higher than 1's. For these students, multiplication tables enabled them to progress beyond that block.

5. *Egg carton multiplication-* Use an egg carton to hold the objects. For instance for the problem 5X3 drop 3 objects into each of five egg carton cups. Then count the number of objects in all.

6. *Boxes of X's-* Materials needed, dice, paper & pencil, tokens. At the beginning of the game players determine how many rounds they will play. The player tosses one die then draws the number of boxes indicated. The same player tosses the die again and put that number of X's in each box and writes the multiplication problem. One turn might look something like this. First roll 3 (draws three boxes) second roll 4 (puts 4 X's in each box) writes problem 3x4=12. The second player follows the same procedure and so on. The player with the highest answer gets a token. The winner of the game is the person with the most tokens.

    1. *Yatzee*
    2. *Flash cards*

Division

1. *Manipulatives-* To make manipulatives for division you'll need small objects (similar to those used for multiplication) and an egg carton, or 3x5 cards. You will use the egg carton cups or the cards to represent the number of sets. Next count out the number of objects you are dividing (dividend) and separate them evenly into the egg cups. (ie for 28 divided by 4- use four cards or egg cups and 28 beans) Then count the number in one pile. For instance 28 ÷4. Place four cards on the table. Now divide the 28 evenly between the four. When you are finished each pile will have 7 beans. So 28 ÷ 4=7

2. *Memorization of facts-* If your child memorizes the multiplication facts, they will have the division facts memorized as well. Sometimes they won't see the connection until you show them. Most of the "tricks" used in multiplication work for division as well.

3. *Magic 9's for division-* Magic 9's for division are the most magical (and easiest) of all! When you divide any number by nine, the answer will be one more than the first digit of

number you are dividing. So 45 ÷ 9 = 5 (which is one more than 4).

Story Problems
There's more than one way to work a story problem. Finding the correct method is half the battle.

1. Play "What do I know"- Write down everything you know about the problem. Next write down what you need to find out. Then decide what operation to use (add, subtract, multiply, or divide). Work the problem. Finally, label your answer and check to see if it makes sense.

2. Make a table or chart
3. Draw a picture
4. Use manipulatives to 'act' it out
5. Work backward from the answer

Another innovative method of solving story problems was created by Donald B Crawford. His program, called *How to Teach Math Facts & Strategies to **All** Students,* was invented with students with L.D. in mind. It simplifies the process by fitting most story problems into either an addition or multiplication format. Though the program takes some training, once the student understands the concept, story problems become a snap.[8]

Memorizing facts
1. *How to Teach Math Facts & Strategies to **All** Students-* This program uses a step-by-step approach that students love, and takes approximately three to five minutes a day. First, students find out how may numbers they can write in 15 seconds, then set goals accordingly. Students progress at their own pace,

---

[8] For more information about this program see Appendix 1 (resources)

learning no more than three facts at a time, and moving on only when those facts are memorized.

2. *Memorization by writing-* This is just what it sounds like and there are several methods. Notice that all three rely on the student thinking or speaking the problem to themselves as they work it. This is *very* important as it gets the information into their brains three different ways, seeing it, hearing it, and writing it.

   A. Write the same problem ten times while saying it to themselves.

   B. Make up a worksheet of between 50 and 100 problems using the same three problems in different order. The student works the problems in order, saying the whole problem to themselves as they write it. Make sure they know all three answers before they start.

   C. Writing an entire set of facts, 2's for instance, over and over again as they repeat the problems to themselves. This helps establish a relation between the problems.

3. *Set to rhythm or music-* For some students a beat will help them memorize. There are several products on the market that set multiplication problems to music. Simply have the student sing along as they write the problems. You can make your own using any music with a strong beat (and no words). Just record the multiplication facts matching the beat of the music in the background. Be sure to use a different song for each set of facts.

Homemade manipulatives and Games

1. *Bean sticks-* Get a bag of dried beans and a supply of Popsicle sticks. Glue ten beans to at least 20 Popsicle sticks. These are the tens. Single beans are used as ones.

2. *Place value charts-* Lay a piece of paper lengthwise on the table and divide it into three equal sections. Make a line about one inch from the top all the way across. Label the far right section "ONES", the middle section "TENS" and the far left section "HUNDREDS". If you need more places follow the same procedure only label the sections "THOUSANDS,"

"TEN THOUSANDS," "HUNDRED THOUSANDS" and so on.

3. *Flash cards-* Use materials that will stand up to rugged "kid" use. Unlined index or recipe cards work well. Simply write the "problem" on the front and let your child write the "answer" on the back. Make sure that the answers are correct and not visible from the front. Many discount stores carry ready-made flash cards of various types which are durable and fairly inexpensive.

4. *Multiplication beads-* You'll need snap-together beads or strings of Christmas beads that you can cut anywhere without losing beads. Snap together or cut strings of beads in groups of two, three, four, and so on. You'll need at least 9 of each grouping, 12 if you are teaching facts to twelve.

Chapter 4

Oral Language

*I knew the way the talk would go
So I entered with a smile,
But the conversation turned on me,
And the day became a trial.
Richard Brubaker (Adult with L.D.)*

Imagine your boss telling you what to do in a mixture of English and Swahili. While you might have a general idea of what he wanted of you, chances are the finer points would remain a mystery. Students with an oral language disability experience this on a daily basis. Often mistaken for discipline problems, language disabilities can land your child in hot water with no clue how he got there.

Language affects everything we do; it is the way we communicate. We use language to process the most basic concepts. All the information we take in through our senses is processed through language. Our very thoughts rely on it. In fact, most IQ tests are language based. If a child has language dif-ficulties, an IQ score may well come out significantly lower that it really is.

Oral language has two parts, expressive and receptive. Expressive language is speaking to others while receptive language is understanding what is said. An oral language disability may affect speaking, understanding, or both.

To understand an oral language disability, it helps to understand how spoken language works. Imagine your brain as a giant information warehouse. For the most part, it is an orderly place divided into cubicles of varying sizes each filled with filing cabinets where bits of information are stored. One of these cubicles is the speech center. The filing cabinets here contain words, each in its own little hanging file and arranged in alphabetical order. When you begin to speak, the retrieval system kicks into gear. Like a well-oiled robotic arm, it opens the correct drawer, locates the proper word, and sends it straight to the speech processor where the words are shuffled into the proper sequence before sending it out your mouth.

Dysnomia is the term for a word retrieval problem. When a child has Dysnomia or an expressive oral language disability, the system breaks down. Everyone has had the experience of not being able to think of a word. It happens when the retrieval system can't find a certain word and has to search for it. That's what an expressive oral language disability is like only on a grander scale. Instead of a neat and tidy file system, imagine one where words are thrown into the drawer helter-skelter. The retrieval system has to hunt for every word, much like trying to find a file that was put back in the wrong place.

Students with this problem may find it difficult or impossible to describe objects or people. One morning at the end of recess, a Kindergartener came into the building crying. When one of my colleagues asked what was wrong, he tearfully explained, "That one kid is picking on me. He hit me with that big thing."

"Which kid?"

"You know, he wears that one coat."

"What does he look like?" she asked.

"He's got eyes and hair and one of those big things."

The teacher tried again. "Can you show me which one he is?"

The boy looked around but apparently didn't see the other child. "I'll show you," he said, taking out a pencil and paper. He drew a circle for a face, triangles for eyes and a frown for a mouth. "There," he said, showing it to the teacher. "Now do you know who I mean?"

Needless to say they never found the culprit. If the Kindergartener had been able to give a detail or two about the other boy's appearance or could tell exactly what the "big thing" was, the teacher might have identified the other student.

If your child tends to refer to "that one thing" or "that kid" rather than using specific names, he or she may have an expressive oral language disability. It is very easy to get a taste of what it's like to have this kind of disability. Just recite the alphabet backward starting with Z.

Time yourself.

Ready?

Go.

Was it harder than you expected? If you had to stop frequently and think about what letter comes next, you experienced an expressive oral language disability. Imagine having to go through the process every time you wanted to have a conversation or ask a question.

Children with expressive language problems have a tough time contributing to class discussions. They'll often raise their hand then be unable to think of what they want to say when the teacher calls on them. Sometimes they'll get in the middle of an explanation and be unable to find the words to finish. The child may have the answer, but the teacher will never know. Figuring out what the student is trying say becomes a guessing game that can leave everyone frustrated.

My fourth and fifth grade language arts class was generating a list of animal nouns one day when Dwayne came up with one he couldn't remember the name for.

"It stands like this," he said, demonstrating with his hands pointed toward each other and his bent elbows cocked out. Then he turned his head back over his shoulder and made a trumpeting noise. The other students and I started guessing. An elephant? Alligator? Crocodile?

"No, no," he said. "It has those things, you know they're hard and grow." He pantomimed a shape growing out of his face.

"A horn?" I asked.

"Yeah."

"A rhino," one of the other kids shouted.

Dwayne shook his head. "No it's got horns on its head."

"Oh, he means one of those dinosaurs," a third student said. "The one with three horns on its face."

"A triceratops?" I asked.

"Yeah, that's it," the others agreed, but Dwayne shook his head again.

"It shoots that stuff out of its eyes when it gets mad."

Now I was really perplexed. "What stuff?"

"That red stuff, you know like when you cut your finger?"

"You mean blood?"

As he nodded, the memory of a book we'd read a couple of months before flashed through my mind, and it all suddenly clicked. "Are you talking about a horny toad?"

Dwayne gave me a big grin. "Yeah that's it!" We had a lively discussion about horny toads, a small horned lizard that is a favorite with local children because it's easy to catch. Since none of us had actually seen one squirt blood from its eyes, we decided it could be an old wives' tale and went on with our animal list, adding elephant, rhinoceros, crocodile, alligator, dinosaur, and triceratops as well as horny toad.

In a resource room, where numbers are small, we were able to figure out what Dwayne was talking about. Though he gave us several wrong clues like the trumpeting sound and the horns on the animal's face rather than its head, we could take the time to work Dwayne through his oral language block. A regular classroom teacher doesn't have that freedom, nor are students like Dwayne as willing to volunteer in a classroom full of students. If they do, they get to the first stumbling block, stop, then say either "I forgot" or "Never mind."

As difficult as an expressive language disability can be, a receptive language disability is just as bad. Students may be able to articulate what they are thinking, but be unable to understand what is said to them.

Several years ago we received a parental referral on a fifth grade girl. Though Sandra was making decent grades, her mother maintained she had no understanding of the material she was supposedly learning. Testing showed a severe language comprehension problem.

So how was she getting such good grades? After only a few days in my class, we knew.

Sandra had been copying off other student's papers, probably since early elementary, and didn't even realize it was cheating. Her receptive language skills were so poor the only way she could follow the teacher's directions was to see what the other kids were doing and copy it. The speech therapist and I collaborated to set up an intensive program for her. Working closely together, we gave her a double dose of vocabulary everywhere we could.

Sandra didn't learn well by listening, but she could learn by seeing and by doing. Once I started teaching her, using visual and tactile input, she began to progress rapidly. In the meantime she was also enrolled in language therapy with the speech/language therapist, working on vocabulary and understanding the language. She had been in the program several months when she said she'd really learned a lot since coming to my class. I told her how much that pleased me, and commented that she'd probably learned even more in speech class.

Sandra looked puzzled. "Not really," she said. "All we do in there is talk and play games. We don't learn anything."

I tried to explain that 'talking' and 'language' were exactly what she was supposed to be learning in speech, but it was obvious she didn't understand. I told Mrs. Stein, the speech therapist, about our conversation.

The next day during speech, the class discussed each game and activity at length. Mrs. Stein explained exactly what they were working on with each game and what they were learning from it. "So," she said when they were finished, "do you understand?"

Sandra nodded. "Yeah."

"All right, tell me what you understand."

Sandra looked confused for a moment then ventured, "We aren't having as much fun as I thought?"

This often happens with a child experiencing receptive language problems. They don't understand what is going on and they don't understand the explanation you give them to straighten it out.

That isn't the worst of it, though. Many students have both receptive and expressive language difficulties. They don't understand what is said to them, and can't tell you where they got lost. They tend to take things very literally. One day Mrs. Stein was working on synonyms with a group of students. As they went around the table, she'd say a word and the student would give her a synonym that meant the same. When she got to Mike, she said the word *scream*. So he did, at the top of his lungs. Then he frowned at her and said, "Why did you want me to scream?"

The *Amelia Bedelia* Books by Peggy Parish are classic examples of a person with this kind of receptive oral language problem. The character, Amelia Bedelia, goes through life doing exactly what her employers tell her to from 'dressing' a chicken in a cute little outfit, to making a 'sponge cake' out of real sponges. Most children find the books very funny. A child with a receptive oral language problem won't 'get' it.

In reality, humor is a higher level thinking skill. Many people with L.D. excel at humor, but not all. The child with an oral language disability has a very difficult time understanding humor. Not knowing when to laugh, or laughing at the wrong time, can make a child stand out and often makes them seem stupid.

Dwayne was a very bright young man, who had many ideas to share. Unfortunately, his language disability kept him from communicating effectively. He had an especially tough time with jokes. One day he came into my room with a grin on his face. "Hey, Mrs. Bru," he said, "do you know why the football coach robbed the bank?"

"I give up," I answered with a smile. "Why?"

"Because he wanted his money back!" He laughed. "Isn't that funny?"

"I don't get it," I said.

He looked puzzled for a minute then confessed. "I don't either."

Andrew, who had walked in right behind Dwayne, shook his head. "That's because it's supposed to be he wanted his *quarter back*."

Dwayne still looked confused. "That's what I said."

It took several minutes for Andrew and me to explain what the joke meant and why it was funny. Dwayne knew what a quarter was and what a quarterback was. What he didn't get was the play on words. He took the language literally.

Just as bad is telling jokes to the wrong audience. When youngsters begin experimenting with humor, about first or second grade, the jokes they tell aren't funny. Then, as they mature, they tend to go through a dirty joke stage when the jokes are funny only because they are completely disgusting or filthy. Imagine a child who tells first grade jokes to fifth graders or sick, dirty jokes to their grandmother. Either scenario is tailor-made to cause embarrassment at the very least and social disaster at the worst.

After the 'quarterback joke' incident, Mrs. Stein decided to do a joke unit with Dwayne's and Andrew's group. Everyday they would take a joke, discuss what it meant, and then learn to tell it. Since Dwayne and Andrew came to my class right after speech, they were supposed to tell me their joke of the day. They were making real progress, especially Dwayne.

Then one day, Dwayne came in all excited about a joke he'd practiced at home. He proudly told it first to Mrs. Stein and then to me. It was a long, involved joke and the longer Dwayne talked the more impressed I was. He had the joke down pat and told it perfectly with all sorts of complex language. I was bursting with pride, when he finally came to the punch line. I'd like to share Dwayne's joke with you.

"A pink man came down the pink highway in a pink car and stopped at a pink motel. He asked for a room so the clerk gave him the first pink room on the left with a pink door and a big pink number one. A little while later another pink man came down the same pink highway in a pink car and stopped at the same pink motel. He asked for a room so the clerk gave him the second pink room with a pink door and a big pink number two. Then another pink man came down the same pink highway in a pink car and stopped at the same pink motel. He asked for a room so the clerk gave him the third pink room on the left with a pink door and a big pink number three.

Bright and early the next morning the maid knocked on the pink door number one and told the pink man they were serving free breakfast in the restaurant. The pink man went to the restaurant and had pancakes. The maid knocked on the pink door number two and told the second pink man they were serving free breakfast in the restaurant. The pink man went to the restaurant and had pancakes. The maid knocked on the pink door number three and told the third pink man they were serving free breakfast in the restaurant. The pink man went to the restaurant and had eggs."

"Do you know what the moral of the story is," he asked.

"No, what?" I said with a big smile.

"Three out of four men prefer waffles!"

Even though it obviously wasn't the right punch line, I couldn't help laughing which, of course, pleased Dwayne no end. "What's with all the pink stuff?" I asked after a minute or so.

"Nuthin'," he said, with a happy grin. "I just wanted the story to be longer."

Dwayne obviously still had a way to go. To this day I have no idea what the punch line was supposed to be, but when

Mrs. Stein and I compared notes later, we decided it couldn't be nearly as funny as we found Dwayne's.

Language problems often cause social difficulties. Because they take the language literally, children with language disorders often don't understand what is being said. As her students left her class, Mrs. Stein often said, "Have a good one."

One day Dwayne waved and said, "Yeah, you too." Then he stopped and looked at her with a puzzled looked on his face. "You always say that. Have a good one what?"

"It means have a good day."

"Why do you say that?"

"It's just a nice thing to say."

"Oh," he said, apparently satisfied. "Well, you have one too."

Though "Have a good one" is not a phrase that could get a student in trouble if he or she didn't understand it, there are many phrases that can. If your child has an oral language problem, you may want to read chapter seven on social problems.

So how do you know if your child has an oral language problem? Though it would take an evaluation to tell for sure, there are some signs that you can watch for.

___ Has difficulty thinking of words.

___ Will often start an explanation, then get confused and says "I forget" or "never mind."

___ Names categories instead of specific words. (i.e. that guy instead of Tom)

___ Has a wide-eyed stare reminiscent of a deer caught in the headlights when they don't understand what you've just said.

___ Doesn't know how to phrase a question.

___ Uses words that sound similar but

don't mean the same thing (i.e. death for deaf).

___ The child takes a long time to process the answer to a question.

___ Talks himself through a question.

___ Very literal- takes everything at face value (i.e. would expect to see a teacher other students described as an old witch carrying a broom and casting magic spells).

___ Uses a description instead of a specific word. (i.e. 'that black and white animal that stinks' for skunk).

___ Answers the wrong question. (i.e. tells you what page he's on when you ask what he's reading).

___ Uses words like *stuff* and *that thing* instead of specific words.

___ Is unable to answer questions when you are sure they know the answer.

___ Struggles to remember information he/she knew the day before.

___ Doesn't understand humor or tells inappropriate jokes.

___ Repeats commercials and funny things he/she hears without really understanding what it means.

You may be wondering what sort of help a student with an oral language problem would receive in a resource program. Though much of the remediation of an oral language problem takes place through a speech/language program, the resource teacher may also be involved.

As the inclusion teacher, it was my job to translate for Dwayne and make sure he understood what was going on in the class. Generally, if I could make him comprehend what the teacher wanted, he could do it. In fact, he had amazing insight. More than once he enabled me to see something from a different point of view and to give me new teaching strategies. One of my favorites is in the Math chapter of this book.

The teacher's job in a pullout program is similar. Whenever I set Sandra to a task, I gave her directions then made sure she understood by asking her to repeat what I wanted her to do. I also made sure she understood key vocabulary and concepts before she began.

Some districts are reluctant to give a child special education services for an oral language difficulty. The perception is that it doesn't really affect school progress. Several years ago I was discussing this with an administrator.

"It's a mistake to place kids with language disabilities in resource rooms. They just keep requiring more and more time," she told me. "By the time they get into high school, they're in resource for everything."

"That's because the farther they go in school, the harder the language becomes," I pointed out. "By the time they get to high school they need a fulltime interpreter. If they don't understand the language, how are they going to understand what goes on in the classroom?"

She had no answer, but I hadn't changed her mind one whit. Unfortunately, many administrators agree with her assessment. Even if the school doesn't see an oral language problem as a learning disability, you can help your child cope with his or her oral language difficulties.

1. When helping with homework, make sure your child understands vocabulary and key concepts. Don't ask, "do you understand what that means?" Often children will think they understand when they really don't. Instead say, "Tell me what you are going to do."

2. Talk to your child as often as you can. In the car, at the dinner table, during commercials on TV. Not only will it keep

the lines of communication open as your child grows older, conversational skills are difficult to learn and present a potential stumbling block.

3. Have your child retell T.V. shows, movies, books, etc. This improves sequencing skills, too.

4. When he or she sees something humorous on T.V., ask your child to explain why it was funny.

5. Watch for a blank or confused expression. Such a look often means your child didn't understand what you mean. Don't hesitate to ask your child if he/she understood what you said.

6. When you give your child directions, check for understanding. Say, "Tell me what you're going to do." Then correct anything he has incorrect or that he's forgotten.

7. Ask your child questions about things he/she has done or seen.

8. Correct mistakes immediately, but do so in a non-threatening manner. Instead of saying "that's wrong," just say "do you mean…" And repeat the sentence correctly.

9. Read to your child often and stop frequently to ask questions. (What do you think is going to happen? What does that mean, etc.)

10. Wordless pictures books help generate great parent/child conversations and help children develop language skill as he/she creates stories to go with the pictures.

11. Have your child repeat important points back to you.

12. Make sure your child uses appropriate details when describing something. For instance if she says, "that one kid" have her tell you specifically who she means. Ask for details like hair color, age, size, name, etc.

13. Teach your child how to ask questions appropriately. This is one of the most common stumbling blocks for a child with a learning disability in the classroom. (You must understand 85% of what you hear to ask a question.).

14. Role play social situations and appropriate conversation.

15. Play name games with your child. One is a variation of 20 questions. The first player says, "I'm thinking of a…" and names a category such as animal or vehicle. The second player gets one guess, then the first player gives another detail about the object. The players take turns thinking of objects and asking questions. This game works well to improve oral language skills as it forces your child to identify specific details of an object.

16. Listening and rhyming games are good language builders.

17. Memory games and bingo boards that entail matching pictures help develop both memory and language skills.

18. Collect a variety of objects and put them in a pile. Then name one detail and have the child sort through the pile for all objects with that detail (i.e. find things with wheels, or everything that is hard, etc.). Return objects to pile then let the child pick a detail.

19. Simon Says- is a good game for following directions and processing information.

20. Defining emotions- Role play or discuss various characters from stories or T. V. programs – "How did they feel? Why?"

21. Occupations- Give details of an occupation and have your child name the community helper (I'm thinking of someone who puts out fires, etc.)

22. There are a variety of language games on the market that kids love to play. Look for those involving categories, naming people or objects, charade type activities, or anything that calls upon your child to use the spoken word. Make sure it is not too frustrating an activity for them.

Oral language problems, perhaps more than any other, can lead your child into confusion and frustration. Sometimes, all it takes is an interpreter to break down the language barrier and open the world of learning.

Chapter 5
Written Language

> I had a story in my head;
> That I couldn't wait to start.
> But words got jumbled in my pen,
> And the whole thing fell apart.
> *Carolyn Lampman Brubaker*

Most of us tend to think of written language in terms of English classes where we identified nouns, learned a zillion grammar rules, and wrote an occasional essay. Many would be hard put to say where they use these skills because the way written language used to be taught had very little to do with writing or with real life.

In reality, writing touches almost every part of our lives. Every time we fill out a job application, write a letter, or send an e-mail, we are judged almost entirely by our written language abilities. Our writing represents us when we aren't there.

During the last few years, there has been a drastic change in the way written language is taught. Many schools now teach written language by having students write as much as possible. Punctuation, grammar, sentence structure, and sometimes even spelling are being taught almost entirely through student writing. Teaching written language skills this way is a definite improvement but presents a whole new set of problems for the child with a learning disability in written language. Often students are expected to write in every class, sometimes even

P.E. Suddenly the student with L.D. is being beaten over the head with his/her disability all day, every day.

There is little similarity between oral language and written language. Both are forms of communications, and both use words. That's about all they have in common. Written language is an entirely different process than oral language. It even takes place in a different part of the brain. Many students with learning disabilities are able to communicate by word of mouth just fine, but when they try to write, it all falls apart. To them, spelling, punctuation, and sentence structure are more mysterious than inner workings of a computer.

Written language is stringing words together in a way that will make sense to other people. While that may sound simple, it is anything but. You can't just write down the words in your head. For one thing, you don't think in complete sentences. Thoughts are more like words and phrases floating among half formed images. It makes sense to the brain but has to be translated into a different form in order for others to comprehend the meaning. To understand how we process written language, let's go back to the image of the brain used in Chapter 4. We can think of the brain as two separate rooms with a firewall between. Both sides contain a huge filing system filled with billions of pieces of information that pass back and forth through holes in the wall. However, the two sides have very little else in common. On the speech side of the brain, words are accessed by a robotic arm dipping into neatly ordered file cabinets and shooting them to the speech center.

The written language part of the brain is very different. Instead of a precision robotic arm, the retrieval system is a whirlwind. Rather than single words, it grabs handfuls at a time and sends them to the written language center to be sorted. The first order of business is to decide which of those words will work the best in the sentence. Then the brain has to figure out how to spell it, whether it needs a capital or not, where exactly it goes in the sentence, what punctuation to use with it, and finally how to program the fingers to write it down or type it. Then the retrieval system has to decide what other words are needed to go with it to get the correct meaning, and the whole process starts all over again. With all of that going on, it's not surprising that some children have a great deal of difficulty with the process. Students with written language disabilities may have trouble in any or all of these areas.

I have developed a simple exercise to give you an idea of what a written language disability is like. First, time yourself as you write out the Pledge of Allegiance, the Lord's Prayer, or some other short piece you know by heart. You will probably accomplish the task within a few minutes without putting too much thought into it.

Now let's try the same exercise as though you have a written language disability. You are going to write your short piece again, only this time you're going to use the following code: A =Z, B=Y, C=X, D=W and so on to Z=A.

Using this code, the beginning of the Pledge would be "R kouwtu…" (I pledge…). It will take you longer, of course, so let's make it fair. After all, most teachers give their slower students extra time. Generally they allow an extra ten minutes or so but I'm prepared to be generous; I'm going to give you *twice* as much time as you need. Before you begin, multiply your recorded time by two. This is how long you have to complete the task. Set a timer and…go…..

Did you have enough time to finish? If not, how far did you get? I'd venture a guess that only a few people could complete this exercise even with double the amount of time it took originally. Having to stop and think about every letter makes the writing process incredibly more complex. In reality, for many children it is even more difficult than the exercise I presented you. Often a written language disability will affect a student's physical ability to write. To give you an idea of the process the student goes through, let's take a trip inside a child's mind to see how this thinking process works.

At the beginning of Language Arts class the first day of school, the teacher asks her students to write a sentence beginning with "One great day last summer…" Johnny L.D.

thinks to himself: "That day I went fishing with Dad and Uncle Jack! That's what I'll write about. Let's see a sentence... One great day last summer, I went fishing with my Dad and his brother Jack."

"All right, *one* that starts with the sound *wu* so that would be a W and you make a W with two lines and a hump in the middle. The next sound is *uh*. That's a U and it looks kind of like a cup. One ends with *n* and that's an N, two lines with a slash between them. Ok, now what was the next word? Oh yeah, *day*...."

Meanwhile the rest of the class has finished their sentences and gone on to the next task. If Johnny does manage to finish, it will probably look something like "Wun da I wint fish Dad and Unkl Jak," which bears very little resemblance to the actual sentence he was trying to write. Imagine living with this kind of a disability in a program that demands you write almost constantly all day. Chances are good that you would quickly fall behind your classmates and would soon lose the desire to write at all.

For most students, coming up with the sentence, remembering what to capitalize and what punctuation to put at the end was all the conscious thought it took. For our little hero, however, the work was just beginning. Once he knew the words he wanted to write, he had to figure out how to spell them and how to form the letters. The process took so long that he lost track of what he was writing. Nor was the end result likely to impress the teacher. Johnny had to work twice as hard to produce half as much.

It's pretty easy to tell if your child is one who has this kind of disability. He or she will do just about anything to avoid writing. My son Paul would rather do his most detested chore than put pencil to paper. If he says, "Hey, Mom, would you like me to mow the lawn?" or "I think I'll go clean my room," I start looking for his assignment notebook to see what he's supposed to be writing.

It's not that Paul lacks the language ability; he had the vocabulary of an eighth grader when he was tested in second grade, and it isn't a lack of ideas. Paul's favorite thing in the world is to make up stories with interesting characters and intricate plots, but when I try to get him to write them down, it's like pushing a string. As difficult as it is for him, I've seen worse.

Several years ago a fifth grader transferred in from another school. He was a rather pleasant boy and I had no trouble with him until we started to write our first story. Suddenly, Ryan was an A-1 discipline problem. It didn't take a rocket scientist to figure out what was going on. Writing was obviously not his cup of tea.

My other students had been with me for a year or two. They knew I made the process as painless as possible and they had even come to enjoy writing. All five of them tried to persuade Ryan he'd like it too. They told him that spelling and punctuation didn't count on this draft, and that they got to rewrite several times before I ever graded it. He wasn't impressed.

I decided to wait, hoping he'd lose his fear as he watched the others writing and having fun. After four days, he was no closer to starting his own story than he had been at the beginning. Finally, I took him aside to have a private word. "I can tell you aren't very comfortable writing," I said, "but I think it's more than that. Would you like to tell what's going on?"

"I can't write," he mumbled.

"Everybody in this class has trouble writing," I told him. "That's why they're in here."

"No," he said, "I can't write."

I gave him a reassuring smile. "It's all right, Ryan, nobody's going to make fun of you."

"No," he said angrily, "I can't WRITE," and made a violent motion like a pencil writing across paper.

The light dawned. "Oh, you mean you can't physically put it down on paper?"

"Yeah," he mumbled with a sullen frown. "The words come out all wrong."

"How about if I act as your scribe?" I asked. "You tell me your story, and I'll write it down."

For the first time I saw hope in his eyes. "You can do that?"

"Sure, why not? This is language not penmanship. I just want you to come up with a story. It doesn't matter if you actually write it down yourself." I opened my notebook, picked up a pencil, and waited. "So, have you given any thought to what you'd like to write about?"

"She came out of the swamp looking for victims," he began, "but instead she became a substitute teacher." The words tumbled out of his mouth so fast I could barely keep up. He never paused until he reached the end, a page and a half later when the unruly students drove Mrs. Gritch back into the swamp. The entire story was there, from the beginning hook to the dynamite ending. The whole time I thought he was goofing off, Ryan had been working on the story in his head.

I never had another minute of trouble with Ryan. In fact, he immediately sat down at the computer and started typing his story. He got so excited about "The Substitute" that he turned it into a book and entered it in the school-wide Young Authors program where he won 6th place. When I returned the book to him after the competition, I made a big deal out of it.

"I want you to take this book home and put it in a special place so you can find it," I told him. "If you ever get to thinking you can't write, this is your reminder that you can. This book not only proves you're a writer, it proves you're a pretty darn good one."

Ryan's problem wasn't a physical one; he could write just fine when he was copying or writing one word answers. The problem only occurred when he had to come up with his own words and write them down. It wasn't a matter of being lazy or unmotivated, either. He really wanted to write that story; he just didn't have the tools to do it with.

There are a number of things you can do for a student like Ryan or my son Paul once you understand the problem. Often it is only a matter of getting the words in their heads down on paper. It's all right for you to act as their 'scribe' and write down what they dictate for anything except a penmanship assignment, when the main emphasis is on the actual writing. Meanwhile there are several activities you can do to help your child develop his or her writing skills:

1. Use a message board for all family members. Small white boards or chalk boards work well.
2. Have your child help with household writing such as shopping lists, party invitations, notes for school etc.
3. Encourage your child to write thank you notes and letters to relatives like grandparents, aunts and uncles, cousins, etc.
4. Don't use writing time to teach spelling. Spell any words your child needs when he/she is writing.
5. If necessary, write as your child dictates. Then, have him copy onto another sheet of paper. This last part is very important. When your child copies what he has dictated, the brain pathways are strengthened and the final product is his own words in his own writing.
6. Teach keyboarding skills as early as possible. Though these children have a difficult time learning the keyboard, once they have mastered it, the computer often solves many of their writing difficulties.
7. If your child has keyboarding skills, there are several different brands of small portable word processors on the market for around $200. They are light enough to carry around from class to class and can hold several different files at once. Later, these files can be printed off or downloaded onto a computer.
8. New speech recognition programs are making it possible to "talk" rather than type information into computers. These programs must be trained to the voice of each user, but are already revolutionizing writing for many individuals when typing is not an option.
9. Older students who have trouble writing fast enough to take notes, can use a tape recorder to tape lectures. Then they can

either take notes at their own speed later, or use the tape in place of notes.
10 If asked to help your child, focus more on meaning than capitalization, punctuation, and spelling. Those things can be fixed later.

Spelling

Though students are beginning to write earlier and earlier in school, spelling is generally the first piece of the written language curriculum that they are graded on. Weekly spelling tests usually begin in first grade somewhere around the middle of the year and last clear into middle school. As one who never passed a spelling test until fourth grade, I know that spelling stands out in my mind as the toughest challenge I faced in elementary school.

To give you an idea of what it's like to have a spelling disability, I'm going to use the tool teachers have used for decades to teach spelling: the spelling test. Since I want to make it fair, I used words you have access to every day. If they don't seem familiar, it's your own fault for not reading the ingredients on the bottles, boxes, and cans your food and medicines come in.

In order to create the real feeling of the disability, use your non-dominant hand to write (left hand if you are right-handed, or right hand if you are a lefty). Now, number your paper from 1 to 9 and have someone pronounce the list below for you. You have a maximum of one minute per word then your 'teacher' will go on to the next. At the end of the test you may ask to have one or two repeated, but if you ask for more than that, your teacher has permission to embarrass you in front of the class by taking you to task for not paying attention. If you are one of the lucky folks who are able to memorize words the first time you see them, don't look at the words before the test.

Ready? Here's the list.
1. Colloidal Silicon Dioxide
2. Croscarmellose Sodium

3. Hydroxypropyl
4. Methylcellulose
5. Methionine
6. Tocopherals
7. Pantothenate
8. Thiamine Mononitrate
9. Pyrodoxine Hydrochloride

It's time to check your work. Remember, if you forgot to capitalize, it's wrong.

So how did you do? If you only missed two or three, you're probably pretty proud of yourself (and with these words you should be). Unfortunately, if you missed more than two, you didn't pass. With only nine words, two wrong is a 77% and three incorrect is a 66%. Most teachers would call that an F.

As humbling as this experience may have been for you, it doesn't even come close to what a youngster with L.D. has to deal with. Pretend you took the test with twenty-five others and most of them passed it with little effort. Some even got 100's and earned little gold stars for their spelling charts hanging on the back wall.

As the year goes on, the charts fill up with stars. Most of your classmates have a handful of empty spaces on their charts, though of course there are three or four that have a star in every square. Determined to be like everyone else, you study and study, but somehow the words never stay in your head. Parent night arrives and your classmates proudly show off their charts, even those who only have four or five stars. Nearly every parent glances at your chart too, then looks quickly away, embarrassed to have noticed it, because yours is the only chart on that back wall as empty as the day it went up. That's the real experience of L.D. and spelling tests. To this day I can't abide gold stars.

The conventional wisdom says, if children are having trouble passing spelling tests in school, they should be studying the words at home. However, it isn't always that easy. For most children, practicing spelling at home is a simple matter of memorization. You know the process. Mom or Dad says a spelling word, Johnny spells it out loud, and by the end of the week he passes the spelling test without too much trouble. Not Sally. Every week her parents helped her practice her spelling words over and over. Memorizing the words was difficult for her, but by breakfast on Friday she could usually spell most them. Three hours later she'd take a test over the same words and misspell eight out of ten.

After two years of this, Sally and her parents all hated spelling. The nightly sessions had turned into battles with accusations of "You're not trying," and "I'm just too stupid to learn," flying through the air. Then one evening, in a fit of angry tears, Sally blurted out her frustration. "They just don't look the same on paper!"

Suddenly, Sally's mother understood the problem. They taught her to spell the words out loud, but her test was written. Because of her learning disability, Sally couldn't transfer her knowledge from one form to another. Sally began taking a written test every evening and then rewriting the words she misspelled five times each.

The process helped, but now Sally couldn't seem to remember the correct spelling from one session to the next the way she had when she spelled orally. Finally her father hit upon the idea of combining both strategies. He told Sally to spell the word to herself as she practiced and then again when she had to write it for the test. It worked! By using three different input strategies, seeing the word (visual), writing the word (tactile), and saying it to herself (auditory), Sally was able to overcome her short term visual memory. She still had a visual memory problem, but she had discovered a path around her difficulty.

Sally's strategy works well for most children. There are, of course, exceptions and other methods that work equally well. Here are a few strategies for you and your child to try:

* Give a written spelling test of the list. Rewrite any misspelled words correctly. Then have the child write the misspelled words five times each, saying the letters to themselves as they write it. Make sure they include the last step. I point out that they are wasting their time if they just write it five times without saying it.

* Break words into smaller recognizable words chunks. "*Together*- it looks like *to get her*." or "*Want*- it has the word *ant* in it."

* If there are no smaller words, break the word into chunks and spell them with a rhythm. In eighth grade I learned to spell the word *decided* using a rhythm. *De- ci-ded*. Sometimes the rhythms follow the syllable pattern, sometimes not.

* *Finger spelling*. Get a copy of the deaf alphabet and teach it to your child. Have him fingerspell the words as he studies. This is most effective with children who are tactile learners.

* *Draw pictures of the words*. Have your child write the words on graph paper with short letters like *a* taking up on square and tall letters like *t* or letter that dip below the line like *g* taking up two spaces. Then draw boxes around each of the letters.

* Have your child type the words on a computer or a typewriter.

The reality is some people will never be good spellers. If a child isn't a proficient speller by the end of sixth grade, chances are good that he/she never will be. I am a prime example. My husband and I probably owned the first hand held electronic spell-checker in town.

An electronic spell-checker is a wonderful little invention that resembles a calculator with a small computer-like keyboard. If you aren't sure about the spelling of a word, simply type it in the way you think it is spelled and press enter. The machine makes a list of possible words and shows them on a small screen. All you have to do is pick the right one and write it down. If you spelled the word right in the first place, *CORRECT* flashes across the screen. Getting a *CORRECT* is an immediate pat on the back, and students love it.

Though I bought the electronic spell-checker to simplify my life, I got an unexpected bonus. It actually improved my spelling! Copying the word from the spell-checker to the page helped me memorize words as nothing else ever has. I first realized this with the word *prairie*. Though it's not a word most people are called upon to spell very often, I use it frequently in the historical fiction novels I write. For some reason, it was a very difficult word for me, and I had to look it up every time I used it. After only a few times of typing it into the spell-checker, I noticed I was getting closer and closer to the correct spelling each time. Then one incredible day, I spelled it from memory. I've been able to spell it ever since. More often than not, the same thing happens to children who use hand-held spell checkers.

Of course, nearly all word processing programs also come with spell check. While they are very handy, and I would fight anyone who tried to take mine away, they don't seem to teach spelling like the hand-held models. The reason for this is simple. On the computer you are given a list of words to choose from. You pick the correct one and press a button. Since there is no interaction with the actual word, no memorization occurs. With the hand-held model you have to write the word down. When the word is written, new pathways are forged in the brain and a memory is created. The next time you try to spell that word, you find that memory pathway and go down it as far as you can. Each time you write the word, the path becomes a little deeper and goes a little farther until you can spell it every time.

When should you buy a spelling checker for your child? A spell-checker becomes a useful tool when the child has enough word recognition to pick the correct word out of a set of similar words, usually about fifth or sixth grade. For some, like my son Paul, that recognition came later. When he hit sixth grade, he still couldn't use one. Often the words he wanted to write were so far above his spelling level that he couldn't get close enough for the spell checker to correct it. Even if he did find the right word, Paul couldn't tell which one from the list it was. I bought him a talking spell checker, and it worked like a charm. He even used it to help him figure out words he wasn't sure of in reading.

So what is the prognosis if your child has a written language or spelling disability? Actually, it's pretty good. In fact, there are many published writers who have written language learning disabilities, myself included. When I speak to writers' groups, I often say I think the greatest invention in the last twenty years is the word processor with spell check. Generally, about a fourth of the audience will nod their heads vigorously while the rest give me a blank look. Writers with L.D. are in the first group. With the invention of the spell checker and the word processor, the field of writing opened up to people who couldn't even dream of it before.

Does that mean your son or daughter will become a novelist? Of course not. But it doesn't mean they won't either. At the very least, they will be able to master the written language enough to get through school and out into the real world.

Chapter 6

Processing Problems and Other Reasons Johnny Can't Read

"A child with L.D. is like a high performance race car you don't have tuned just right. When you find the right combination, it will take off and beat all the rest!"
Richard Brubaker (Adult with L.D.)

Many leaning difficulties are caused by processing problems. A processing problem is the brain's inability to process certain kinds of information. Sometimes it's an input problem, and sometimes an output problem. In other words, the difficulty may stem from the way the brain interprets information coming in or from the way the brain puts information out. The child who reads words backwards, can't remember the teacher's directions, or struggles to write the simplest sentence may well have a processing problem. Some of the symptoms of a processing problem are:
* Difficulty communicating with words
* Having difficulty expressing themselves in writing
* Poor spelling
* Difficulty identifying individual words
* Difficulty discriminating between sounds
* Poor reading skills including decoding and comprehension
* Difficulty listening or following directions
* Hearing words incorrectly

* Using incorrect words that sound similar to the correct word (death for deaf)
* Doesn't always know right from left
* Difficulty learning simple physical tasks such tying shoes or buttoning clothing
* Reversing letters (b for d) and words (reads was as saw)
* Saying words or letters move, disappear, blur, change, or are distorted
* Seeing colors or lights when trying to read
* Using a finger or a marker to keep his place when reading
* Poor handwriting
* Difficulty using mathematical symbols, or sequencing steps to solve a mathematical problem
* Difficulty lining up numbers, one under the other, when writing math problems
* Difficulty understanding new concepts

Though some states don't consider a processing problem a learning disability, to my way of thinking, processing problems are the epitome of a learning disability. Because of the brain's inability to process information in a "normal" fashion, the learner is forced to use a different method to learn. In other words, "they learn differently."

There are some processing problems that are readily diagnosed. The most common of these are Central Auditory Processing and Scotopic Sensitivity or Irlen Syndrome. Both are input problems that can impact a child's learning dramatically, and neither is obvious to most teachers.

As the name implies, Central Auditory Processing deals with information that comes in through the ears. It isn't a case of not hearing well; in fact people with a Central Auditory Processing problem (or CAP) seem to hear too well. Many lack the ability to block out the extra sounds that come in.

Imagine, for instance, a child with a Central Auditory Processing problem sitting in a class. He can hear what the teacher is saying just fine. However, he also can hear the kid behind him tapping his pencil, the heater fan blowing, a car going by on the street, someone sneezing out in the hall, and the girl three rows over tearing a page out of her notebook equally well. It is nearly impossible for such a child to sort the teacher's voice out of the din.

It's fairly easy to give yourself an idea of what it's like to have a CAP difficulty. Take every radio, tape player, television, CD player, and DVD player that you own into the same room. Turn all the volumes up as far as they will go, making sure each is playing something different. If you have a limited number of such noise-makers, you can get the same effect by turning on your blender, exhaust fan, garbage disposal, food processor, and dishwasher all at once. Now, sit down and try to have a conversation with someone clear across the room. Imagine trying to learn in such an environment. Unfortunately, for many students with CAP, the average classroom is just as noisy.

Teachers often find children with CAP problems highly distractible. In fact, they are frequently misdiagnosed as having Attention Deficit. They may have a great deal of difficulty following oral directions, taking notes, or participating in class discussions. Spelling and phonics are often very tricky for children with CAP problems. Most can't tell the difference between the *i* in *sit* and the *e* in *set*. In fact, *cup* and *cap* may even sound the same. Imagine trying to sound out a spelling word if half the letters sounded the same to you.

A CAP evaluation is usually done in a sound-proof booth by an audiologist. There are several different tests involved, and it generally takes about an hour. The results for each ear are usually recorded as percents with 100% being normal. Say a child had 60% in the left ear and 95% in the right. That basically means she hears and understands 60% of what goes into the left ear and 95% of what goes into the right. Obviously this is a student who should sit with her right ear toward the teacher. This is a simplified interpretation, of course, but gives you an idea of the kind of information a CAP evaluation might reveal.

Courtney transferred into our school at the beginning of third grade. She had been tested at her previous school and placed in the resource room for reading and written language. It wasn't long, though, before we began to notice some problems that didn't seem to be covered by the IEP. She had a tough time following oral directions and often responded to questions with a blank look. When the annual review came around, the team discussed the problem. We suspected an oral language problem but the testing didn't support it. Our speech therapist had little experience with the test that the other therapist had given so we decided to do some testing of our own. The new test results were similar to that of the former district. We scratched our heads and rewrote the IEP for another year.

By the time Courtney's three-year re-evaluation came up the next year, she was floundering in math. She couldn't seem to grasp new concepts and didn't have a very good understanding of concepts learned in pervious years. We were even more convinced she had an oral language problem; everything pointed to it.

As part of her re-evaluation, Courtney was given a full battery of tests including in-depth oral language and math assessments. When we compiled all of our assessment data we were scratching our heads again. A third speech therapist with an entirely different set of tests still found nothing significant, and yet the symptoms of a language impairment were more obvious than ever.

About the same time, her mother took her to an audiologist for a Central Auditory Processing test. When we got the results of Courtney's CAP test, the light came on. She had a 50% Central Auditory Processing deficit in each ear. No wonder Courtney appeared to have language problems; half of what she heard wasn't getting processed through her brain. Though we couldn't "cure" Courtney's CAP difficulty, we now knew what kind of help to give her.

Some school districts have the facilities to test for CAP; others will pay for an outside evaluation if there is a strong indication for such testing. Should you tell the teacher if you suspect a CAP problem? Definitely! Even if the testing is not available, there are a variety of accommodations teachers can make for students with CAP difficulties. Many of them will be helpful to you at home as well.

* Gain the child's attention before talking- make sure he or she is looking at you and listening to what you are saying.
* Give directions one at a time using precise language.
* Check for understanding of directions. For example you might say "Tell me what you're going to do."
* Encourage your child to ask for clarification.
* If asked to repeat directions, try to paraphrase using short, clear sentences.
* Give frequent breaks if possible.
* Some teachers will provide a written copy of oral direction or notes given in class.
* If your student needs to take notes in class, a tape recorder may be useful.
* Preferential seating in the classroom. This is usually closest to where the teacher most frequently teaches, i.e. the front row. It should also be as far away from auditory distractions, like doors and windows, as possible.
* Sound attenuating muffs like those used on rifle ranges may be very useful during study periods. Some students prefer foam earplugs to cut down extra noise.
* The use of a sound system where the teacher wears a microphone in the classroom is often helpful. If your school has some classrooms with sound systems and those without, you may want to request your child be placed in a classroom that has one.

Another type of processing problem that is easily diagnosed is Scotopic Sensitivity Syndrome (SSS) commonly know as Irlen Syndrome. SSS is to the eyes what CAP is to the ears. The brain has difficulty interpreting what it sees. People with Irlen Syndrome may see a variety of distortions when trying to read. Some report blurring of print, flashes of light or color, words moving or disappearing or running together, weird spacing between words, lines flowing off the side of the page, and letters and words reversing themselves (b for d, and saw for was). Others complain of headaches, light sensitivity, tired eyes, falling asleep when they try to read, poor night vision, and problems with depth perception.

So what exactly is Irlen Syndrome? The syndrome was discovered in the early eighties by Helen Irlen, a school psychologist. She found that some people with moderate to severe reading problems were helped by placing a colored plastic overlay over the text. During the subsequent years her research has shown that approximately one in five people has some degree of the syndrome. Ms. Irlen developed a screening procedure to identify those individuals and find the appropriate overlays for them to use. She has also developed a diagnostic test to prescribe tinted glasses. [9]

The treatment for Irlen Syndrome is so simple detractors don't believe it could really help. For most people it is a sheet of colored plastic laid over the print or wearing a pair of tinted glasses. The screening process determines what color or colors of overlays work best. The diagnostics for glasses is more complex but essentially uses the same principle.

For some reason not yet understood, reading through the colored plastic sheets cuts down the distortions, making it possible to read. You can see why many teachers scoff at the idea. If it's that easy, why haven't we been doing it? I'll admit I was a bit skeptical myself when I first heard of it. Then an Irlen diagnostician came to my hometown to train Irlen screeners. They needed volunteers to practice on, so my husband Richard and our son Paul went to be screened. When they came home, Paul had three purple overlays and Richard had one blue/gray and two turquoise overlays.

---

[9] If you want to know more about Irlen Syndrome, <u>Reading by the Colors: Overcoming Dyslexia And Other Reading Disabilities Through The Irlen Method</u> by Helen Irlen is an excellent resource.

L.D. From the Inside Out

I might not totally trust a child who told me reading through a piece of blue plastic was easier because kids are so impressionable, but my husband is a natural skeptic. He went into the test thinking he read just like everyone else. His whole perception changed when the screener laid the turquoise overlay on the page and he suddenly saw something he'd never seen before. All the words on the page were in focus at the same time! He says what he normally sees is like smearing butter over a sheet of glass and leaving a one inch circle of clear glass in the middle then laying it over the page. That's the way he had always read. Until he saw the page through the overlay, he had no idea that what he saw was any different than what others saw. Not surprisingly, he reads only for short periods of time and tires quickly.

Richard's testimonial made a believer out of me. Right then and there, I decided to learn how to identify Irlen Syndrome. Statistics say about 20% of the population is Scotopic, and I had the feeling many of my students with L.D. were in that 20%. As it turned out, about 90% of my students tested positive for Irlen syndrome, though not all chose to use the overlays. Some people, including my son Paul, get a glare on the overlays from overhead lighting and are unable to use them to read.

There are different degrees of involvement, of course, and what each person experiences is different. My daughter is light sensitive and sees some minor blurring on the page. Another young woman's whole world was so distorted, she thought doorways were shaped like a set of parentheses.

David was the first client I ever screened for Irlen Syndrome. At the time, he was a twenty-year-old college student, so I wasn't expecting anything unusual when I asked him what happened when he read.

"Well," he said. "The page looks like a big round bowl with the lines of print moving around it in a circular motion. After a few seconds the middle of each word glows and disappears. Then when I begin to read, the line below gets bright and gobbles up the words that I'm trying to read."

I was stunned. "How in the world did you ever learn to read with all that going on?"

He shrugged. "When I was a sophomore in high school I had Mononucleosis and had to stay in bed for six weeks. I got tired of watching T.V. so I worked at reading until I finally figured it out."

The most amazing part of this story is that none of David's high school teachers knew he couldn't read. Many of them didn't even know he had a learning problem. He is one of the most gifted people I have ever known. He also has the most severe learning disabilities. Did the overlays cure David's learning disabilities? Of course not, but they did make it easier for him to read.

At the end of 4th grade, my son Paul tested at a beginning 3rd grade level in reading, which was almost two years behind. Since he couldn't use the overlays, we decided to try the tinted glasses. Paul was fitted with Irlen filters at the beginning of 5th grade. I admit I was hoping he'd immediately be able to read, but it didn't happen. The glasses didn't cure his Scotopic Sensitivity; they didn't even cure his reading problems. They did, however, get the distortions out of his way so he could learn to read.

Paul's reading gradually improved until he took the standardized test at the end of his fifth grade year. This time he tested out at 5.8 (5th grade 8th month), a dramatic growth of nearly three years in nine months! It wasn't only the glasses; he also had excellent teachers. Still, since the school was departmentalized, and he'd had those same teachers in 4th grade, I'd say the glasses made a significant contribution to his growth.

So how do you know if your child has Scotopic Sensitivity Syndrome? The only way to be certain is to have your child screened by a certified Irlen Screener. Some school districts have such a person on staff, and some districts even screen all children when they start school. However, because knowledge of Irlen Syndrome is relatively new, many professionals have never heard of it. Luckily, there are a steadily increasing number of Irlen clinics around the country. The Irlen website at www.Irlen.com has a list of them. If you contact a clinic near you, they should be able to provide you with the name of a screener in your area.[10]

Following is a list of symptoms that may indicate Irlen Syndrome. No one has all the symptoms. If your child has five or more, you may wish to have him or her screened for Irlen Syndrome:

___ Is sensitive to bright light
___ Prefers to read in dim light
___ Avoids reading of any kind
___ Avoids reading books, prefers magazines or newspapers
___ Avoids reading magazines or books with white glossy pages
___ Complains of headaches
___ Eyes get red and watery when reading
___ Eyes get dry and sandy when reading
___ Eyes hurt, ache, or burn when reading
___ Tires easily when reading
___ Has a difficult time reading under fluorescent lights
___ Squints or blinks frequently when reading
___ Gets nauseated or sick to the stomach when reading
___ Skip lines or words when reading
___ Rereads lines
___ Inserts words from line above or below
___ Frequently loses place when reading

---

[10] Contact information for the Irlen Institute is included in chapter 15

___ Easily distracted when reading
___ Uses a finger or other marker to keep place while reading
___ Moves reading material closer and/or farther away while reading
___ Has difficulty lining up numbers in math problems
___ Has difficulty staying on the line when writing
___ Has difficulty reading certain colors of ink on white boards
___ Doesn't understand what is read (poor comprehension)
___ Doesn't remember what is read
___ Takes frequent breaks when reading
___ Gets restless or fidgety when reading
___ Words blur, move, or change, when reading
___ Sees bright lights or flashes of color when reading

If you suspect Irlen Syndrome, you should get your child screened as soon as possible. The overlays or tinted lenses are the best accommodation for the problem, but there are things that you can do at home to help. The following list of accommodations is similar to those suggested at the Irlen website at Irlen.com. A list of accommodations for teachers may be downloaded from the site.

Colored Plastic Overlays: An Irlen plastic overlay can be used over reading material, especially with white or high gloss paper, under fluorescent lights. As mentioned earlier, a screening for Irlen Syndrome will identify the appropriate color or colors. You may also wish to check into Irlen filters (tinted lenses).

Paper Color: Experiment with different paper colors. Often a student with Irlen Syndrome has difficulty with worksheets printed on white paper. You may wish to investigate the color of ink which is most readable with colored paper as well. If you discover a paper that works well for your child, tell the teacher so he/ she can print all your child's worksheets on that color. You may even want to buy a ream of paper for the teacher to use. It is a small expense and makes a nice gesture, especially since school budgets are tight and many teachers don't have access to colored paper. If you make such an arrangement, be aware that the teacher may not be able to use the special paper all the time.

Lighting Conditions: Experiment and find the area in your home where the lighting conditions are most comfortable for your child to read and work. Avoid fluorescent lighting if possible. Indirect natural lighting and incandescent lighting are the best. Dim lighting is usually better than bright lights, though not for all. Some individuals with Irlen Syndrome actually prefer bright working lights.

Breaks: Incorporate breaks into reading, writing, or other homework tasks.

Bookstands: A bookstand is often helpful to a student with Irlen Syndrome. Sometimes the position of the reading material affects glare and distortions caused by bright lighting. Some people find if useful when copying from one place to another as well

Markers: Some students like to use a ruler or book marker when reading. It may be used in a variety of ways. Students find it helpful to place a marker under the line; others place it on top of the line; or after the word being read to block off the rest of the sentence. By isolating the words, a student is able to cut down interference from the line above, the line below or the words that come after. Sometimes the color of the marker makes a difference too. If possible the marker should be the same color as the plastic overlay. Many teachers try to discourage the use of markers or fingers. If your child needs this accommodation, tell the teacher your child has a tracking problem and needs the marker to keep his/her place while reading.

Brimmed Hat or a Visor: Many students benefit from wearing a visor or hat with a brim when reading. The brim shades the eyes from bright lighting.

Be sure to read chapters 2, 3, 4, and 5 for more accommodations to try in reading, math, and language.

As I mentioned before, a processing problem is to me the epitome of a learning disability. It makes learning through normal channels downright difficult if not impossible. In some states, a processing problem automatically qualifies a youngster as having a learning disability, and in others, a processing problem *must* be identified for a student to be labeled with L.D. Ironically not all states recognize processing problems as learning disabilities. In fact, in my home state of Wyoming, processing isn't even mentioned in the rules and regulations.

Whether or not your school provides services, it is important to recognize if your child has difficulty processing information. Though there is no cure for processing problems, knowing about them goes a long way toward understanding your child's learning disability.

Though not considered processing problems, there is another group of terms in the family with L.D. that get lots of press. Whenever learning disabilities are mentioned, someone will usually come up with the term Dyslexia. A great deal of research is currently going on in the field with some rather surprising results. It was recently discovered, for instance, that some Dyslexics appear to use the speech center of the brain to read with rather than the portion "normally" used. If that's true, it means reading for a Dyslexic takes place in a completely different part of the brain, one that deals with spoken language rather than the interpretation of symbols. It's sort of like being born without hands and learning to use your feet in place of them.

It should be noted here that many people diagnosed with Dyslexia may also have Scotopic Sensitivity Syndrome and the accommodations made for SSS work for many Dyslexics. In fact, some Dyslexics' symptoms disappear when they use an Irlen plastic overlay.

Although Dyslexia is the most famous, there are others just as common and just as hard to deal with. Here the names and definitions of several.

Dyslexia: A severe difficulty in understanding or using one or more areas of language, including listening, speaking, reading, writing, and spelling.

Dyscalculia: A severe difficulty in understanding and using symbols or functions needed for success in mathematics.

Dysgraphia: A severe difficulty in producing handwriting that is legible and written at an age-appropriate speed. Also a severe difficulty in producing written language.

Dysnomia: A marked difficulty in remembering names or recalling words needed for oral or written language.

Dyspraxia: A severe difficulty in performing drawing, writing, buttoning, and other tasks requiring fine motor skill, or in sequencing the necessary movements.

Though you and your child may well be dealing with Dyslexia or one if its brethren, you may not hear it from the school. As a special education teacher, I am frequently asked if I can test for Dyslexia. In reality, there isn't any one test that can identify Dyslexia or any of the others for that matter. An accurate diagnosis involves a multifaceted evaluation including neurological tests as well as a wide variety of academic testing, only part of which is the traditional IQ test. School districts simply aren't equipped to do such involved testing, nor do they have the experts who could interpret the results. For this reason many schools don't even use the terms.

Even experts in the field of Dyslexia hesitate to use the label for individual students. The difficulty covers such a wide spectrum of difficulties that it is often best to just describe the symptoms. It makes more sense to say that Suzy reverses certain letters and often has trouble tracking than to simply say she has Dyslexia. A teacher would have an idea how to attack Suzy's specific reading problems, but really wouldn't know where to start with the diagnosis of Dyslexia.

I've even heard very knowledgeable educators insist that Dyslexia doesn't really exist. In reality, as far as education is concerned, it doesn't. If you tell the school your child has been diagnosed as Dyslexic, don't be surprised if they brush it off or even tell you there is no such thing. Instead, be prepared to tell teachers what your child's processing strengths and weaknesses are. They will find the information much more useful in dealing with your child.

Besides, labeling a child Dyslexic isn't nearly as important as what to do about it. Neither Dyslexia nor any of the others can be cured. However, like most learning disabilities, they can be overcome, though it may well entail a long and difficult fight. People with Dyslexia can become voracious readers, and those with Dygraphia, like this author, can become writers. You will find useful strategies to use as weapons in the battle in chapters 2, 3, and 5, on reading, math, and written language.

There are a great many books on the subject of Dyslexia and its relatives as well as a variety of organizations that deal with the problems of Dyslexia. Some are listed in chapter 18 but more can be found by a search on the Internet or a trip to your local library. Local Parent Training Centers[11] or Parent Information Centers (PICs) may also be able to provide you with information and resources.

---

[11] **For more information on Parent Training Centers see chapter 14. Parent Training Centers in your area are listed in chapter 15**

Chapter 7

Social Skills

> I never go to parties,
> 'Cause I'll do something wrong,
> And I hate to look the fool,
> In a merry-making throng.
>
> I always seem to talk too much,
> Sometimes I stand too close.
> It's when I'm with a crowd of folks,
> I hate L.D. the most.
> *Carolyn Lampman (Adult with L.D.)*

Of all learning disabilities, social skill difficulties are the hardest to deal with and by far the most painful. More than any other kind of L.D., it results in isolation and rejection. Social skill issues will make a child stand out as learning disabled far quicker than academic difficulties.

Many people with learning disabilities don't read social clues and often react in inappropriate ways. Some children can't even tell when a teacher is angry by reading body language or facial expressions. Others don't understand how to dress appropriately, when not to tell off-color jokes, or when to stop talking. Many don't realize that what is appropriate in one situation may not be in another. Behavior that is perfectly acceptable in grade school isn't in Jr. High, for instance, and you don't talk to your principal and your friends the same way. Often people with L.D. don't understand the unspoken rules of society and are ostracized because of it.

I recently saw the results of a poll conducted among adults with learning disabilities. The participants had been asked to rank various areas of their life in order of difficulty. Social skills came in a surprising second right after education. Adults who had lived with learning disabilities all their lives considered surviving in society almost twice as difficult as getting and keeping a job!

Though at first glance this may seem odd, it really isn't difficult to understand. As an adult, most things you don't do well can be avoided by your choice of profession. If you have difficulty with math, for instance, you don't apply for jobs that entail working with numbers.

Social situations, however, cannot be avoided. Every interaction between two or more people is social. Even going to the grocery store or attending a movie involve certain rules of etiquette. You know, for instance, that you don't select items from someone else's grocery cart, even though technically the groceries don't actually belong to them. Nor would you crowd to the front of a line to purchase your movie ticket or buy popcorn. Chances are no one ever told you that; it's just something you picked up as a child by watching the adults around you.

These 'invisible rules' are taught by example, and most children learn them easily. Unfortunately, many children with learning disabilities don't learn by example. In his video, *Last One Picked, First One Picked On,* Richard Lavoie talks about the skills necessary for a child with L.D. to survive in a mainstream classroom. Lavoie asked teachers at all levels what skills a child needed to possess in order to be successfully mainstreamed. Across the board teachers identified the same seven skills.

The student needed to be able to:
1. Listen
2. Follow directions
3. Stay on task
4. Know how to ask for help

appropriately
5. Get started on his/her own
6. Finish on time
7. Read the material

Of the seven, only reading is taught in school. The other six are invisible rules teachers expect their students to know. Schools are full of invisible rules. Some are academic; others like how to line up after recess, and raising your hand to talk, are survival skills.

Take, for instance, the concept of personal space. It is never taught and rarely even mentioned. Unlike math, reading, or even manners, personal space is not a straight-forward set of rules. What are acceptable changes from culture to culture, from situation to situation, and even from age to age. A very dif-ferent set of rules applies to toddlers than to teens.

Nearly all of us have had the experience of standing shoulder to shoulder with a complete stranger in an elevator. While not particularly comfortable, it isn't threatening in any way. Now, imagine getting into an empty elevator and pressing the button for your floor. Before the door closes, a stranger gets on and stands right next to you. Suddenly, you are extremely uncomfortable and very threatened. Your personal space has been invaded.

Most children learn this concept early on. Babies and toddlers often smile at strangers and will sometimes even grab a leg or hand of one. By the time they reach three, they have become somewhat more wary and shy. Most have a fairly well developed sense of it by the time they get to school. If they don't, the results can be devastating.

Jimmy was a bouncy little boy with a spattering of freckles and a winning smile. Though most adults thought he was an adorable child, when Jimmy got to school he couldn't seem to make friends. By first grade, teachers were beginning to see him as a troublemaker. By third, his classmates avoided Jimmy and picked him last for any game even though his size and athletic abilities were above average. As the isolation and peer rejection started to take their toll, Jimmy became sullen and introverted.

Concerned, his parents turned to the school for help. The school social worker discovered that Jimmy didn't have a clue why kids reacted to him the way they did. In fact the friendlier he tried to be, the more they rejected him. His peers, on the other hand, reported many incidences where he intimidated them with his superior size. Most were leery of Jimmy, and avoided him when possible. Teachers complained that he was always bothering the other children and taking others' belongings. Nobody wanted to stand next to him in line because he shoved and pushed those around him. He was perceived as a bully on the playground since he was constantly tripping, poking and bumping into other kids as well as taking playground equipment others were using.

One afternoon the social worker observed him in gym class. As he watched Jimmy pushing his way between two teammates, he suddenly realized the boy had no notion of personal space. What other students perceived as intimidation was nothing more than Jimmy getting too close. Nor did he understand about personal property. To him a pencil was a pencil. It didn't matter if it was his or someone else's; if he needed it, he used it.

To help Jimmy understand the concept of personal space, the social worker set up an activity with Jimmy's class. Each child took a turn standing still while others walked up to him. The child told the person approaching to stop when they started to get too close. The social worker laid down a circle of string around each child showing his or her comfort zone, in other words, their personal space.

Afterward, the social worker took Jimmy aside and talked about the exercise, pointing out how he was violating the other kids' personal space. They practiced walking up to each other and stopping the right distance away. They also discussed personal property and role played the proper way to borrow materials from other students. As Jimmy's social awareness increased so did his social acceptance.

Our world is full of "invisible rules" fully complex as personal space. Anyone who moves to a different region of the country needs a period of adjustment to learn all the "invisible rules of survival" of a place. For instance, in my home town we experience very harsh, cold winters. We have dozens of ways of coping, from leaving twenty minutes early on snowy mornings, to running a trickle of water to keep the pipes from freezing when the temperature dips to forty below zero.

Several years ago, a family moved in from the South. Because our winter survival skills are second nature, no one thought to tell our newcomers any of it. By the time spring arrived, they were packing to move. Many of our youngsters with learning disabilities are just as confused and lost. Imagine how hard school would be if you didn't know the appropriate time to sharpen your pencil or to use the restroom. What if you didn't even know the right way to ask a question? Far fetched? Not really. Youngsters with L.D. are quite often considered trouble makers or branded as discipline problems because they do appropriate activities at inappropriate times and have no concept of why they are in trouble.

My first year of teaching, I had a first grader named Mickey. One afternoon he got up and walked out of my classroom without a word. He was astonished when I came after him and stopped him in the hall. "Just where do you think you're going?" I asked in my best 'teacher' voice.

He was clearly surprised. "To the bathroom."

"You know better than that," I said sternly. "You're supposed to ask first."

"I am?" His eyes were filled with confusion as he looked up at me. "But I already know where to go. My other teacher showed me." Since he was new to the school environment, he had no concept of asking permission for things he did at home whenever he wanted.

Two years ago I had a third grader new to the school. The first time I let Gina go to get a drink, she was gone for nearly ten minutes. The next time, I said she had to be back in five minutes or lose the privilege. She came back to my room several minutes later escorted by a teacher who said, "I caught her running in the hall. She says you told her to."

"It was the only way I could get back in time," Gina told me tearfully. "Last time I walked, and you said I was too slow."

It couldn't be true, of course. The drinking fountain was just down the hall from my room. Yet something about the earnest way she said it made me think she was being completely honest. Thinking perhaps she was having trouble with the drinking fountain somehow, I told her to show me how she got a drink.

To my surprise, we didn't go directly to the drinking fountain. We walked right past it and all the way down the hall to Gina's third grade room. Then we turned around and headed back. By the time we finally arrived at the drinking fountain I understood the problem. Gina only knew how to get to the drinking fountain from her third grade classroom. She passed it every day on the way down to my room and even stopped to get a drink occasionally. But because she was looking at the hall from a different perspective when she came from the other direction, Gina didn't recognize where to turn.

Mickey didn't understand the invisible rules of school, and Gina didn't know the physical layout. Like the skills needed for successful mainstreaming, neither is taught in school yet teachers and parents alike assume children understand them. Even though neither Gina nor Mickey purposely disobeyed, they were both in trouble, and neither of them knew why.

So how do you prepare your child for everyday challenges like these? First of all, make sure your child is ready for new situations before they occur. Visit the school before school starts and help your child locate the classroom, the bathrooms, drinking fountains, gymnasium, lunchroom, etc. Practice getting to all of them from various places, including the playground.

That goes for non-school activities as well. One of my most vivid memories happened when I was six years old. We had moved to a new town. The first time I went to Sunday school I remember going through a confusing series of Sunday school classes to a small room down in the basement next to the kitchen. I didn't have a clue how we got there. Because it was shorter, the teacher took us out through the kitchen at the end of class. As a result, the only way I knew how to get to my Sunday school class was through the kitchen, a path I used quite happily for several weeks.

One morning the door was locked, and I didn't know where else to go. I sat there by the door and cried for what seemed like hours. Someone finally came to the door and let me in, but scolded me with a stern warning never to use that door again, as it wasn't for children. Since I didn't know any other way in, I stopped going to Sunday school. My parents never understood why, and I never explained because I thought I'd done something terribly wrong by going through the kitchen. If someone had made sure I knew the appropriate way in, the whole situation could have been avoided.

It is equally important to prepare the situation for the child. Visit with your child's teacher and find out exactly what his/her rules are for going to the bathroom, sharpening pencils, etc. If your child has a problem in this area, you may want to alert the teacher, without making a big deal out of it. Be sure to present it in a non-demanding manner. The old saying about catching more flies with honey than vinegar is especially true here.

It's also important to find out just what the teacher's expectations are. This is especially true in the upper grades. Say your child has two teachers. One is a stickler for promptness while the other is more concerned that students come prepared for class. If your child discovers he has forgotten a book or homework assignment, it is imperative that he knows what each teacher wants. The one will be angry if your child takes the time to go to his locker for the book. The other will be equally angry if he doesn't. Similarly, some teachers base a big part of their grades on homework and less on tests. Others use homework for learning new skills, and base grades on tests. Students need to know which is which.

In general, there are some skills you can teach your child that are sure-fire teacher pleasers. Number one on the list is an oral language problem. Many students with learning disabilities don't know the appropriate way to ask a question or request more information. Flopping the paper down on the teacher's desk and saying "I don't get this," or "I can't do this" doesn't cut it. Teach children to identify exactly what it is they don't understand. "I don't understand where to write my answer," or "I'm not sure exactly how to do the next step" or even "I don't quite understand how to work this problem."

Following is a list of other teacher pleasing strategies that can have a significant impact on the way your child's teachers perceive him or her.

* Be on time to class (Line up as soon as the bell rings)
* Have all supplies and materials ready when you need them
* Participate in class discussions.
* Establish eye contact when listening to teachers as well as when talking to them.
* Turn assignments in on time.
* Call teachers by name instead of saying "Hey Teacher".
* Say please and thank you.
* Smile and say hello.
* A good morning and a good bye will go a long way toward good teacher-student relations.

Generally, the best solution is to anticipate trouble before it happens. If you have an idea of what kinds of problems your child may face, it is possible to prepare him or her for the situation. Also be sure to let teachers, coaches, Scout masters, 4-H leaders, and other adults working with your child know about difficulties they may run into. If warned in advance, most adults won't ask your child to do something he or she may find difficult. There may even be times you can give other adults an insight that will help them work with your child.

I happened to be at the swimming pool one day when the coach was trying to teach my youngest son the back stroke. Paul had the moves down, but no matter what the coach said, he kept turning the wrong direction and wound up face down in the water every time. After practice, I took the coach aside

L.D. From the Inside Out

and explained that Paul's learning disability kept him from understanding what she was telling him to do. Between the two of us, we came up with a solution. Whenever Paul had trouble learning a new stroke, the coach physically took him through the motions. Once he knew how the stroke was supposed to feel, Paul was usually able to do it on his own. When he learned to ski, we used the same technique with the ski instructor and she had him whizzing down the slope in no time.

Below is a list of skills that can impact social situations. As you go through, place an Y on the line in front of those skills your child has and a N in front of the skills your child does not have. Once you have completed that, make multiple copies and your social skills list is ready to use.

Each time your child enters a new social situation, go through the list and check off each skill that will be needed in that situation. Those that have Y's next to them are the strengths that will help your child steer a safe course through the reefs of social interaction. Those with both check and minus signs are problems areas that may cause difficulty. For example, if a child were getting ready to join Boy Scouts, a portion of his list might look something like this:

Needed for this activity	Has this skill	
x	Y	Gets along well with children the same age
_	Y	Gets along with family members
x	Y	Gets along well with adults
_	Y	Gets along well with younger or older children
x	N	Makes and keeps friends
x	Y	Easily adjusts to new situations
_	N	Keeps track of materials

A quick glance identifies potential problem areas, in this case getting along with the other boys in the troop. It also shows possible solutions. Since he gets along well with adults and adjusts quickly to new situations, a visit with the scoutmaster before the first meeting might be just the ticket to make him feel more comfortable.

Now suppose the same child decides to go to summer camp. Though we start with the same basic checklist, the final product looks rather different.

Needed for this activity	Has this skill	
_x_	_N_	Gets along well with children the same age
_	_Y_	Gets along with family members
_x_	_Y_	Gets along well with adults
_x_	_Y_	Gets along well with younger or older children
_x_	_N_	Makes and keeps friends
_x_	_Y_	Easily adjusts to new situations
_x_	_N_	Keeps track of materials

Notice that getting along with older or younger children and keeping track of materials were not important in the first situation. Suddenly, those skills are very important. Since summer camps are usually multi-aged, you might consider sending a sibling or an older friend along to help ease the way.

Now that you understand the checklist, take a few minutes to fill it out. In the interest of space, expla-nations have been kept short. If you find a term you are not sure of, check the glossary for a definition. Remember, when filling out the checklist, place a star on the line in front of those skills your child has and a - in front of the skills your child does not have. At the end there are blank spaces to add other skills as you think of them.

L.D. From the Inside Out

Social Skills Checklist

Activity_____ Date_____

Needed   Has
for this   this
activity   skill

____ ____	- Gets along well with children the same age
____ ____	- Gets along well with adults
____ ____	- Gets along well with younger or older children
____ ____	- Gets along with family members
____ ____	- Gets along well with teachers
____ ____	- Makes friends
____ ____	- Keeps friends
____ ____	- Works well in a group
____ ____	- Is easy to get to know
____ ____	- Easily adjusts to new situations
____ ____	- Asks questions appropriately
____ ____	- Answers questions appropriately
____ ____	- Is able to make understandable explanations
____ ____	- Focuses on a task long enough to finish
____ ____	- Has a good imagination
____ ____	- Good short term memory
____ ____	- Good long term memory

___ ___ - Memorizes easily
___ ___ - Understands wrong and right
___ ___ - Takes responsibility for his/her own actions
___ ___ - Can read well
___ ___ - Can write
___ ___ - Can do grade level math
___ ___ - Is truthful
___ ___ - Can sit for long periods of time
___ ___ - Understands spoken directions
___ ___ - Understands written directions
___ ___ - Shows respect for authority
___ ___ - Completes what he/she begins
___ ___ - Is able to organize his/her possessions
___ ___ - Is able to organize his/her time productively
___ ___ - Has a good sense of humor (age appropriate)
___ ___ - Is athletic (can catch a ball etc.)
___ ___ - Dresses appropriately for his/her age
___ ___ - Is not easily frustrated
___ ___ - Enjoys learning new skills
___ ___ - Understands and can tell jokes appropriately
___ ___ - Likes challenges
___ ___ - Stays calm under stress
___ ___ - His/Her feelings are

___		not easily hurt
___	___	- Has good self-confidence
___	___	- Thinks before he/she speaks
___	___	- Does not blurt answers
___	___	- Does not say inappropriate things at the wrong time
___	___	- Is not shy
___	___	- Can read body language
___	___	- Cares about neatness and accuracy
___	___	- Takes criticism well
___	___	- Has good fine motor skills
___	___	- Has good gross motor skills
___	___	- Doesn't mind being away from home
___	___	- Understands what is "in style" and what is not
___	___	- Accepts praise appropriately
___	___	- Is not clumsy
___	___	- Does not mind being touched by others
___	___	- Can connect emotionally with others
___	___	- _____
___	___	- _____
___	___	- _____
___	___	- _____
___	___	- _____
___	___	- _____
___	___	- _____

Now that your checklist is complete, you may wish to make several copies to have available when you need them. Because each situation is different, you will need a new checklist each time your child approaches a new set of circumstances.

Another very useful tool is the *instant replay*. Even with all the preparation in the world, children will still make mistakes. Don't look upon these as failures, but rather as teaching opportunities. If used in a positive way, *instant replays* can be powerful tools. The child frequently won't understand what they did wrong and will often do the same thing again. Though it is tempting to *tell* the child what he did wrong, it is more effective help him dissect the incident, figure out what went wrong, and then brainstorm other ways he could have handled the situation.

You may find the problem came about because your child misinterpreted something that was said. Many social problems are caused by an inability to understand the language. If your child has ever told you he or she got in trouble at school but honestly doesn't seem to know why, chances are good it was a case of misunderstanding the language.

Several years ago, a fellow teacher came to me seething with frustration. "You're going to have to go get Lisa if you want her to come down today. She's sitting outside my room in a snit."

"Lisa?" I was startled. Lisa was a quiet little mouse of a girl who rarely spoke. I couldn't imagine what she could have done to make her teacher so mad. "What on earth happened?"

"I sent her to the office with the daily attendance at eight-thirty. When we traded for reading groups at eight-forty-five, I found her standing outside the door. She hadn't even taken the attendance folder to the office yet."

"Why not?" I asked in surprise.

"I'm not sure; she refused tell me. The more I questioned her, the more stubborn she got." My colleague shook her head. "I couldn't even get her to come down to you."

"All right, I'll see what I can do," I told her, wondering what in the world was going on. The child Mrs. Barry described was nothing like the Lisa I knew.

I found Lisa right where Mrs. Barry had left her, sitting on the floor by the classroom door with her head down on her knees. I sat down next to her. "What's going on?" I asked.

"Nothing."

I tried again. "Are you having a bad day?"

She nodded. "Mrs. Barry yelled at me."

"Oh? What for?"

Lisa gave an audible sniff. "'Cause I didn't take the attendance to the office."

"Why not?"

"I didn't know how."

"What do you mean you don't know how?" I asked in surprise. "You take it down all the time."

"Yeah, but she wanted me to do it differently today."

"Different how?"

"She said to put my best foot forward." Lisa looked up at me with red, tear-drenched eyes. "I don't know which is my best foot."

Lisa had been confused by what she thought were instructions. Because she was shy and lacked appropriate question-asking skills, she didn't know how to ask for clarification. She knew she was in trouble but didn't have a clue why.

If your student frequently gets in trouble and really doesn't seem to know what he or she did wrong, you may be dealing with an oral language disability. You will find information on oral language disabilities in Chapter 4.

To recap, below are some skills to help your child avoid some of the invisible social pitfalls of a new situation in school and out. As with other learning disabilities your child probably won't have all the difficulties described. Still, it might be a good idea to check and make sure he or she understands everything in this section. Sometimes children have developed strategies that make them look like they understand when they really don't.

1. Make sure they know the physical plan of the school. This goes for all buildings they must access, as well as the route to and from school (or the bus stop).

2. Don't assume your child knows something because it's common knowledge to the rest of the world.

3. Role play appropriate social behavior with your child. Often telling them how isn't enough; he or she may have to be shown.

4. Teach teacher pleaser skills.

5. Teach the appropriate way to ask a question or request more information.

6. When your child is entering a new situation, try to anticipate problem areas and help prepare you child to meet them.

7. When appropriate, prepare the situation for the child as well.

8. Don't view mistakes as failures. Use them as learning tools.

9. Do instant replays of social mistakes to insure your child understands what went wrong and how to prevent it from happening again.

Though social skills are for many the most difficult of all learning disabilities, your child doesn't have to flounder in a sea of social mistakes. With a little prevention, some training and a whole lot of support, your can conquer the complex world of society and its rules.

Chapter 8

ADD & ADHD

> They were dwelling on spelling,
> and where was I?
> That was then I chose
> To watch the....
> I'm sorry, what was the question?
> *Louis R. Lampman*

Ready....Fire.....Aim. These three words are the best description I have ever heard for ADD and ADHD. Attention Deficit Disorder (ADD) and Attention Deficit Hyperactive Disorder (ADHD) are two of the most popular 'buzz' words in education today. ADD and ADHD are not considered Learning Disabilities, but the two often go hand in hand. In fact, the incidence of ADD and ADHD in the population with L.D. is almost double that of the population as a whole.

ADD and ADHD are typified by poor attention span, high distractibility, and in the case of ADHD, hyperactivity. Though the terms are often used interchangeably, ADD, and ADHD are very different from each other. To illustrate the difference let's take a look at my three sons. All three have learning disabilities, but Jason also has ADHD, Leroy has ADD, and Paul is just a very active child.

Recently, Paul's science class dissected cow eyes. To get everyone's attention at one point in the procedure, the teacher said, "All eyes up here." Paul later confessed he had a momentary urge to take the teacher literally and throw his partially dissected eye toward the front of the room. A second later, he realized the teacher would not find it particularly humorous and didn't act on his impulse. That's the reaction of a normal, active child.

Jason, on the other hand, is the epitome of impulsivity. The moment the idea flashed through his mind, the eyeball would have been airborne. That's ADHD.

Leroy, my laid-back son, is about as far from hyperactive as you can get. He would have missed the whole 'eyeball' incident because he wasn't paying attention and didn't hear the teacher's direction in the first place. That's ADD.

Of the three, Jason spent the most time in trouble with his teachers, Leroy got the poorest grades because he missed half of what went on in class, and Paul had the most entertaining stories to tell about school.

Of course this definition doesn't always hold true. Not all children with ADHD bounce around like a super ball. I, for example, have ADHD. Though I've learned to do it in undetectable ways, there is a portion of my body moving at all times even when I sleep. However, people who knew me as a child would describe me as very quiet and shy. Even now people have trouble believing I have ADHD unless they watch me do housework. For some reason, I've never quite been able to organize that part of my life the way I would like. If you want to take a peek at ADHD from the inside out, read the beginning of Chapter 10. I started out to record a morning of chores and wound up with a classic ADHD demonstration.

Attention Deficit isn't new; it's been around as long as man has. It's only been the last few generations that it's been considered a handicap. In fact, in the past it was often a positive. Imagine, if you will, a hunting party of cavemen roaming the tundra looking for game. They discover a baby mammoth and go in for the kill. The youngster's terrified cries attract its mother. Suddenly, the tribe is under attack by a full-grown mammoth, and the men clamber up a nearby rock wall to escape.

As they watch helplessly, the enraged mother grabs one of their number from his precarious perch, dashes him to the ground and reaches for another. Out of the blue, Gronk gets an idea. Without another thought, he jumps from the rock wall onto the mammoth's head and stabs his spear into the animal's eye. Several more stabs into the brain bring death to the huge animal and a hero is born. At the celebration feast, Gronk is given his choice of the meat and lauded as one of the greatest men of the tribe. No one suggests that he take medication for his unfortunate tendency to act without thinking.

Many of our great heroes appeared to have Attention Deficit tendencies. Teddy Roosevelt's charge up San Juan Hill during the Spanish American War was classic. It was a great victory against overwhelming odds, a tribute to American guttsiness, and a really dumb thing to do! Or what about George Washington deciding to cross the Delaware on a bitterly cold Christmas Eve? It was such an unlikely thing to do that the Americans took the enemy by surprise, captured their objective, and escaped back across the river before the rest of the British army even knew they'd been there.

Once you know the symptoms you'll find examples all through history. I caught the tail end of an old WWII movie recently that retold a true story of the war. A small group of Americans wound up facing what looked like half the German army with only a tank and their rifles. Artillery fire took out the tank almost immediately, and the Germans charged. An American soldier, Audie Murphy, jumped onto the burning tank, grabbed the machine gun, and started firing. The other Americans stayed where they were, horrified at what he was doing. Not only was the tank full of gasoline and ammunition, it was on fire and ready to explode! Wave after wave of Germans came across the field, and he mowed them down, apparently oblivious to the fact that he was standing on a ticking time bomb. The last of the Germans fell, and he jumped down from the tank just as it blew sky high.

An epilogue to the movie told that he'd been awarded several purple hearts and a Congressional Medal of Honor among others. Yet, Audie Murphy constantly refuted the idea that he was a hero, maintaining he wasn't any braver than anyone else. Perhaps he was just being modest. On the other hand, it may be that he didn't see himself as a hero because he didn't do what he did out of bravery, but because he didn't stop to think first about how foolhardy it was. It's impossible to know, of course, but I have my suspicions.

If you go back to my original definition, of *Ready...Fire...Aim,* Audie Murphy certain appears to fit the description. Any one of those soldiers could have done what he did, but they took that extra moment to think and realized it was almost certain death if they did.

Audie Murphy, Teddy Roosevelt, George Washington, and even Gronk were true heroes, of course, and I don't mean to take anything away from their heroic deeds. My point is, that like most learning disabilities, there is a positive side to ADHD and ADD that we tend to ignore in schools.

Why have ADD and ADHD been around so long? Scientists and doctors have long suspected a genetic link to ADD and ADHD. If that's true, it's easy to see how it gets passed down from generation to generation. Our caveman, Gronk, probably had no trouble finding a mate; the women were all enthralled with his bravery. His genes were almost certainly passed on to the next generation and the next.

My own family appears to illustrate the point and not just because my brothers and I all have ADHD. In recent years I have dabbled a bit with genealogy. I started with my great grandparents who homesteaded in the West in 1887. My great grandfather had experienced several setbacks in Iowa, so he hopped in a wagon and headed for Wyoming to take a look around. He never went back.

At the beginning of the Civil War, his father, my great-great grandfather, tried to enlist in the Union army. When he was turned down because of poor health, he loaded his family in a wagon and headed west to Iowa. So it goes generation after generation clear back to the early 1698 when they were kicked out of Germany for being religious dissidents. That was when my great-great- great (etc.) grandfather loaded his family on a ship and headed west to America.

On the other side of my father's family, I discovered a pilgrim ancestor. Though he came over on the Mayflower with the rest, Edward Doty was not your typical pilgrim. The first time history mentions him is when he participated in the first duel in the New World; one combatant used a cutlass and the other a knife. Clearly not a well-thought-out venture. In later years he was convicted of slander, disorderly conduct, assault, stealing firewood, and letting his cows eat the neighbor's cornfield. It's pretty obvious that impulsivity was his besetting sin. The first time I read about his misdeeds I looked at my husband and said, "You know, I think ADHD has been in my family for a very long time." If I were able to go back far enough, I have no doubt I'd find Gronk or someone just like him on my family tree.

Though scientists aren't yet positive what causes Attention Deficit, most agree it is a chemical imbalance. According to the theory, the nervous system of people with Attention Deficit lacks the proper amount of Dopamine, the chemical responsible for transmitting impulses between nerves. Without the proper amount of this 'neurotransmitter' the nerve impulses can go astray. While some of them do get to the proper nerve ending, many go zinging off into the great beyond.

It's kind of like the difference between filling a bucket with an open hose and filling it with a sprinkler. As you hold the hose in your hand, water pours out in a full stream that is easy to direct and quickly fills the bucket. Now try it with a sprinkler. No matter how you hold it, only part of the water gets into the bucket. The rest goes off in a dozen different directions.

When you think of those stray water jets as nerve impulses, it's easy to see why people with ADD and ADHD are so easily distracted. Each one of those little streams represents a different focus and a potential distraction. It is difficult for a child with an Attention Deficit to stay focused on one thing when so many others are begging for attention. My brother Rush, who also has ADHD, says it's more like firing a shotgun in the air then running out with a bucket and trying to catch the B-B's. I think, perhaps, his ADHD is a bit worse than mine.

Often highly active children are classified as ADHD when they may not be. That's why a medical doctor needs to be involved in an ADD or ADHD diagnosis. Generally, parents and teachers will be asked to identify behaviors that point toward ADD and ADHD. Several different behavioral checklists have been developed to help with this task. Once parents and teachers have filled out a checklist, the results are tabulated and ranked on a scale.

It is not unusual for school results to be very different from the information gathered at home. In fact, it is quite common for mothers and fathers to rate the child quite differently. When we filled out the questionnaire on our son LeRoy, I found him much more distractible than my husband did. Upon reflection, we realized that I was more likely to do the sit down, quiet, homework type activities with him than my husband was. By the same token, his reading teacher ranked him as much more distractible than his P.E. teacher.

The checklist does not definitively prove whether children have ADHD or ADD, but it will indicate if they have difficulty paying attention and if they are overly active. With some children it is easy to tell, while others are borderline. Only a medical doctor can determine what medication, if any, should be administered. Whether to medicate or not depends on the individual child and is a difficult decision to make for many parents.

The medication, most commonly Ritalin, works like an artificial Dopamine in the body, enabling the nerve impulses to travel across the synapses from one neuron to another. Unfortunately, Ritalin has gotten some bad press in the last few years. Since I am not a pharmacist, a medical doctor or a scientist, I can not speak to the risks or side affects. I can only share experiences of my own children and those of some of my students with you.

I heard the term ADHD for the first time when my son Jason was in third grade. He had been given a psychological evaluation as part of his three-year re-evaluation. The psychologist diagnosed him with classic ADHD and described him as someone who burns his bridges before he gets to them, then fords the creek.

When the psychologist read the official definition to us, I swear it sounded as though the author knew my son personally. Jason moved constantly, did really stupid things without thinking, and generally caused havoc wherever he went. If quiet surrounded him, he filled it with noise. Even so, we were reluctant to put him on medication because no one really knew what the long term effects might be.

As Jason grew, so did his problems. The older he got, the more trouble he had finishing his school work and following school rules. He seemed to constantly be in trouble and was driving his teachers crazy. Finally, after three years of fighting it and at the end of our rope, we decided to try Ritalin. The results were remarkable. Suddenly he had friends and some of his teachers actually liked him. He still got into trouble occasionally but not nearly as often and his grades improved. Jason will always be impulsive, but with Ritalin he was able to focus on his work and to control most of his annoying habits.

Jason's case is not unique. Several years ago I had a student who could have been a poster child for ADHD. If Julie forgot to take her Ritalin, I could tell within the first ten minutes after she walked into the classroom. Without her medication, Julie was a jet-powered ping-pong ball, bouncing around, making all sorts of noise and completely unable to focus on anything for more than a few seconds at a time. It was impossible to hold her attention long enough to teach her.

Unlike Jason, Julie seemed to need to take her medication consistently over a period of time for it to have any effect. Uncomfortable with the whole idea of giving their daughter Ritalin, Julie's parents discontinued the medication during the summer. Every fall Julie came back to school and went back on the medication. The first week was always pure torture for everyone involved. After one morning with Julie, the calmest, most even-tempered teacher I have ever known was ready to throw in the towel.

Worst of all was the way it affected Julie. It was nearly impossible for her to function either in the regular classroom or in the resource room. She spent the first few weeks of school every year bouncing in and out of trouble, unable to focus and producing next to nothing. As the resource teacher, it was my job to convince her new classroom teacher that Julie did indeed belong in that particular grade and that she would eventually come around. In the meantime, Julie was faced with frustration at every turn.

As soon as she started taking Ritalin again, things gradually began to improve. Even so, it was always November before she settled. By then the first quarter of school was over and she'd missed a significant amount of learning time.

On the other end of the spectrum is the child with ADD. While ADHD tends to make itself known immediately, ADD is often difficult to identify. Unlike the child with ADHD, the student with ADD may appear calm, even sluggish. While we were still trying to get Jason's ADHD under control, my husband attended a seminar on Attention Deficit.

The speaker, a nationally known expert in the field, talked about both ADHD and ADD. It was the first time we'd ever heard that the two were distinctly different. Richard came home convinced that we needed to take a look at LeRoy, too. Though he had none of Jason's hyperactivity, he was something of a space cadet. He rarely remembered his homework, and even if he did, he'd forget to turn it in. His locker was full of half-finished work. Some assignments he started three or four times and finished none of them.

Having learned our lesson with Jason, we requested an evaluation by the school district. All of LeRoy's teachers were given checklists to fill out. Many thought it was ridiculous to consider attention deficit for such a laid-back kid, but most of them filled out the checklists anyway. The results were surprising. When all the checklists were tallied, LeRoy was more distractible than 80% of his classmates. That means out of ten seventh graders, eight of them were on task more often than LeRoy.

We felt it was significant and so did the doctor who prescribed a light dose of Ritalin. LeRoy's reaction was even more pronounced than Jason's. He actually remembered to do his homework, and even got it turned it in. Within a few weeks, his grades went from D's and F's to A's and B's.

Without my experience with LeRoy, I probably wouldn't have recognized Logan's problem when I had him as a student several years later. You would never have picked him out as a child with an attention deficient. He was rarely a discipline problem, never shouted out answers and didn't show an excess of motion. His only problem seemed to be that he never got his work done. It took forever to get him started on an assignment. Even then the teacher would have to get him back on task every time she came by. The work he didn't finish in class went into his desk and was never seen again.

At first I thought it might be a language problem. A child who does not understand the language will often not begin an assignment because he doesn't know what to do. Once someone comes along and explains the directions, though, such a child is usually able to do what is asked of them. Logan seemed to know *what* to do; he just didn't do it. To the classroom teacher, he appeared lazy and unmotivated.

Logan was far from motivated, but the more I thought about it the more I wondered if there might be another cause. In my smaller setting, I'd seen him work diligently for awhile then sort of drift away. I'd also seen him pulled off task by another student asking questions, someone walking by in the hall, the heater switching on and even a slight buzz from the wall clock.

I began keeping track of his off-task behavior. What I found surprised me. Though he wasn't disruptive, Logan was off-task more than half the time. His inattentive periods varied from a few minutes to half an hour. I felt it was significant enough to warrant further investigation. His parents agreed and we did the checklist. Sure enough, he came out highly distractible though his score for hyperactivity was below normal. A medical doctor reviewed the information we provided along with his own findings and prescribed Ritalin.

Almost immediately we began to notice a difference. Suddenly Logan could complete his assignments with few if any reminders and even began to finish ahead of some of his classmates. His grades began to improve too, though not as profoundly as LeRoy's. Logan still had trouble remembering to turn in his homework and occasionally had several copies of the same paper stuffed in his desk, but the Ritalin did make an enormous difference in his life.

Is Ritalin or drugs like it the only answer? Of course not. Some parents, reluctant to put their children on prescription drugs, have experimented with various herbal and dietary regimes as well as coffee and high caffeine soft drinks. I can't speak to the effectiveness of any of these, since I have never had any experience with alternate methods. You may wish to explore some before making any decisions about what is best for your child.

There are many books, articles and web sites devoted to ADD and ADHD. A visit to the library and a search on the Internet will provide you with a great deal of information. A visit with a physician may be enlightening as well. If your doctor is not an expert on Attention Deficit, he can probably direct you to a colleague who is.

Occasionally when a child begins taking Ritalin, they complain about the way it makes them feel. Doctors are usually at a loss to explain this, and it often passes as the child begins to adjust to the medication. Since I didn't know I had ADHD until I was an adult, I never took Ritalin as a child. Perhaps my experience will shed some light on why children don't like to take it.

Several years ago I needed to straighten up a set of shelves in my classroom before summer vacation. They covered one entire wall, and I knew it would be a horrendous task. I put it off until I could avoid it no longer. I hadn't had much experience with Ritalin yet, but I knew it helped me focus on the task at hand, so I took one and set to work.

I started at 8:30 and worked steadily until I finished. Not once did I get distracted or leave my task. I didn't look at the clock while I was working, but I was aware of time passing. After what I thought was about three hours, I stepped away, proud and pleased with all I had done. Imagine my shock when I looked at the clock and saw that it was only 9:30 instead of 11:30!

For a person with Attention Deficit, life races along at a break-neck pace. Time slips away with incredible speed, and you never seem to finish anything. It's an unfathomable mystery how others can be so much more efficient and organized. The day I cleaned that shelf was the first time in my life I experienced the passage of time the way everyone else does. It was truly enlightening.

So why do kids hate to take it? From an adult perspective it was great; I suddenly had two extra hours to get things done. But look at it through the eyes of a child. Chances are he or she is on Ritalin because of difficulty in school, and it's probably not a favorite place to be. Suddenly time begins to creep along; it takes twice as long to get through the day. No wonder they object.

I rather like some of the effects of Ritalin. After all, I can get my work done in a timely fashion and still have time left over. Imagine being given an extra hour or two every day. Still, I don't take it on a regular basis. I have spent my life dealing with ADHD and have many strategies that help me cope. Perhaps I would feel differently if I had grown up using Ritalin. I can almost guarantee my housekeeping skills would be better.

Regardless of whether you decide to use drugs or not, there are some things you can do to help your child deal with Attention Deficit. A list of them follows. It is divided into two sections, one to help with organizational difficulties and one to deal with impulsiveness and annoying mannerisms. The many books and internet sites dedicated to Attention Deficit will have more. As you experiment, you and your child will find others that work.

Organizational tools

1. Rote memorization is an effective survival skill for some, though not for all. Teach step-by-step procedures for any new activity then practice until your child has it memorized.

2. Establish specific routines where ever possible. Sticking to a routine helps a child focus on the job at hand. (Chores, getting ready for school, doing homework etc.)

3. Create step-by-step checklists for activities not done on a daily basis (cleaning a bedroom, for instance)

4. Make lists of tasks you expect your child to do, then gradually shift the responsibility for making the lists to the child.

5. For older students or adults a day-planner can be lifesaver.

6. Other tips can be found in the chapters on Chores and Homework.

Dealing With Impulsivity

1. When your child is faced with a new situation, role play and practice appropriate behavior.

2. Time-out. Though this is often used as a punishment, it can be far more valuable as a positive intervention. Establish a time-out area and use it as a place to calm down, or cool off. If time-out is used this way, many children will begin to time themselves out when they start to lose control. I have found it very effective in the classroom as well as at home.

3. If your child is one that needs to move constantly, have him/her use body movements that are unobtrusive and quiet. Instead of tapping a pencil on the desk, for example, I drum my fingers on my thigh. When that isn't possible, I wiggle my toes. No one even notices.

4. Individuals with Attention Deficit often don't realize when they annoy others. Make your child aware of irritating mannerisms in a nonjudgmental, matter-of-fact way. Then set up a code so you can quietly call your child's attention to inappropriate behaviors without embarrassment.

5. If your child tends to talk too much, impulsively blurt out, or interrupt, teach appropriate conversational skills. Then practice, practice, practice. Over-learning is a very effective tool for teaching these skills.

6. Build appropriate movement into activities that require long periods of staying still. For example, my son Jason would take a break and run two laps around the outside of the house while he was doing homework. We started with fifteen minute work periods and gradually worked our way up to forty-five minutes.

Chapter 9

Homework

"Being L.D. means working twice as hard to get half as much done."
Richard Brubaker (Adult with L.D.)

For a student with learning disabilities, homework can lengthen an already too long school day to nightmarish proportions. The kids aren't the only ones who feel that way. To this day my mother-in-law shudders when you mention the word. When my husband was in grade school, they tackled homework together every night, and every night they both ended up in tears.

I'd like to tell you that my own homework encounters were considerably different, but they weren't. Even with all my experience as a teacher, I found helping my own children with homework frustrating, irritating, and downright difficult. I've even been known to say that I can teach any child except my own!

The first thing you have to do as a parent is give yourself permission to have trouble working with your child. Not only is it normal, it's almost a given. If you don't have these problems, give yourself a pat on the back and say a quick prayer of thanksgiving because you are definitely in the minority. That said, there are ways to make homework less painful for everyone involved.

One of the most difficult parts of the homework question is knowing when there is homework to do. Good communication between home and school can often mean the difference between a student who succeeds and one who fails. Logan, a student with ADD couldn't seem to get his work finished. Ritalin helped but still his homework seemed to fall into a black hole somewhere between home and school. He rarely remembered work he had to finish long enough to take it home, and if he did, it would usually disappear before it ever got back to school. For four years he had his teachers and parents pulling their hair out. If they sent work home, it never came back. If they kept him in from recess to work, he'd get the assignment started but it would disappear into his desk when the bell rang and never see the light of day again.

Things were just as bad at home. Every night Logan's parents asked if he had homework. Every night he said no, because as far as he knew he didn't. The paper that occasionally got home and finished often never made it back to school. Frequently a note came home detailing missing work that Logan's parents distinctly remembered him finishing. Logan would be sure he handed it in, so another note would fly back to school questioning if the teacher had lost it. Often as not it lay moldering away in his backpack or his desk. Meanwhile, his grades were floundering.

Logan's parents, the classroom teachers, and the resource teacher tried a variety of things, but nothing seemed to work. Finally, through trial and error they came up with a workable system. Armed with a daily planner, Logan checked in with the resource teacher every morning. If he'd forgotten his planner, she gave him an assignment sheet. During every class he wrote down his assignments. If he finished one, he checked it off and had his teacher initial the planner. At the end of the day the resource teacher checked the planner, made sure he had all his assignments and books and then added her own initials to the page. When he got home, his parents checked the book, then initialed it themselves. Any papers that were finished went into a special folder to be turned in first thing in the morning. The next morning the whole process started all over again. It worked. Though Logan still lost an occasional paper, most of his homework got finished and handed in.

If you decide to use a planner, make sure that everyone involved buys into it, including your child. All it takes is one person who forgets to sign it for the whole thing to fall apart. It's pretty natural for kids to fight the idea, but usually they will give in when they see the parents and teachers are going to hold firm. As soon as the lines of communication are opened, it becomes second nature for parents, teachers and students to write in the planner every day. If your student finds a planner too difficult to keep track of, daily assignment sheets can be used instead, but you still have to make sure that everyone signs it.

A planner doesn't work for everyone, however. In fact many students with learning disabilities find it too cumbersome. Others, like my son LeRoy, never seem to have it where they need it. He'd tell the teachers it was at home, and tell us it was at school. Sometimes a small reward will take care of that problem. Julie, for instance, got a small sticker every time she got it home. She could trade the stickers in for privileges like an extra half an hour before bedtime. It was all she needed to help her get the planner home. If you find that a reward system does not make an appreciable difference, it may be that a planner just won't work for your student. Most often it is because they can't keep track of it.

My son Paul was one of those. This was a child who would miss lunch because he forgot he had a check for lunch money in his backpack. On top of that, writing was such an ordeal for him that recording assignments in his planner took much longer than anyone else; time he could ill afford to waste. Then a teacher came up a quick and simple solution. During each class the special ed paraprofessional wrote the assignments in Paul's planner for him. As for the tie to home, a weekly assignment sheet came in the mail at the end of the week. Each teacher listed the assignments Paul was missing. At first he had three or four a week, but by the end of the first year it was down to one a month. Since the object was for Paul to get homework done not for him to record assignments, it worked quite well.

Many students will come up with their own method of keeping track of assignments. The following are some examples that you and your student may like to experiment with.

1. LeRoy finally hit upon the idea of using a five-subject spiral notebook. He especially likes the ones with pockets in the dividers to hold handouts he gets in class. He uses a different section for every subject with a page at the beginning of each dedicated to assignments. When he finishes an assignment, he checks it off. At the end of every day all he has to do is check each section to see what he needs to take home.

2. George uses a stack of spiral notebooks, one for each class. They are color coordinated so he can remember which is which. Whenever the teacher gives an assignment, he writes it down on the first page in that notebook. When he does his homework, the assignment and work he already has finished on it are right there in the appropriate notebook. When he gets to class the next day, he opens his notebook, tears out his homework and hands it in.

3. Margaret could never keep track of multiple notebooks so she relies on her textbooks. Whenever a teacher gives an assignment, she writes it at the top of her paper before she even begins to work. When class is over, she folds her paper in half and sticks it in the textbook with about and eighth of an inch showing. At the end of the day, she grabs the books with papers sticking out of them. It is an easy matter to pick up where she left off when she gets home.

4. Paul uses a homework folder. Like Margaret, he writes the assignment at the top of the page before getting down to work. He also dates the paper so he knows what day it was assigned. At the end of class he sticks the paper into his folder. When it comes time to do homework, he opens the folder and looks for things dated that day. This is also handy when a teacher asked about a specific assignment. He only has to search the homework folder instead of his locker, his back pack, all of his textbooks, his bedroom, or the kitchen table where he did his homework.

5. Kay carries a zip-up binder. At the end of every class she sticks unfinished work in the front of her notebook. When she gets home at night, all of her homework is at her fingertips as soon as she opens her notebook.

6. Beth tends to lose things like planners and notebooks. If she has an assignment, she writes it on the palm of her hand. She claims it's the best place since she's never once lost her hand and if she ever does, homework will be the least of her worries!

7. Josiah has a rough time with high school block scheduling. He couldn't remember which classes were on which day and as a result never knew which homework to do when. He solved his problem by investing in two distinctly different looking backpacks. One is his even-day pack and the other is his odd-day pack. He keeps both backpacks loaded with everything he needs. On even days he carries the blue backpack all day long, sticking assignments in it as he goes. At the end of the day he takes it home and does all the homework for that day, while it is still fresh in his mind. The next morning he throws the blue backpack in his locker and grabs his red one, which contains everything he'll need for that next day including his homework. Nothing goes back and forth between the two packs. He's even gone so far as to buy two small dictionaries and two calculators. Josiah admits it's a rather expensive solution but it was worth every penny.

8. At the end of class Wayne sticks unfinished homework papers in his pants pocket. That way no matter what he does during the day and after school, his homework makes it home with him. He admits he doesn't have the system perfected yet since papers do occasionally get lost or washed, but I have no doubt he'll refine it into a workable method before long.

Difficult as it is, getting the homework home is only the beginning. The real battle begins when it's time for your child to sit down and do the work. Many parents have a difficult time getting their children going on homework. With kids who have learning disabilities L.D. the confrontation is likely to be even worse. Put yourself in the child's shoes for a moment. You spend the whole day struggling to do work that your classmates seem to race through. You're working as hard as you can but never finish anything before the teacher tells you it's time to put your books away. No matter how hard you try, it's never enough, and you wind up feeling frustrated and stupid time and again.

At last the day is over and you can go home. You're exhausted but looking forward to kicking back in front of the T.V. and relaxing. The minute you walk in the door, your mom asks if you have homework and says you'd better get to it. Suddenly your backpack, which is stuffed with all the work you didn't get finished in school, weighs a ton and the evening stretches before you in an unbearable echo of the day. Is it any wonder that students with L.D. tend to rebel?

Several years ago my husband came up with a solution that worked extremely well for us. Every afternoon I set an alarm clock for seven P.M. Nobody even mentioned homework until it went off. When my children got home from school they had three or four hours to play with their friends, watch T.V., talk on the phone, play computer games, or do whatever they wanted to. At seven o'clock the alarm rang and the homework came out. Even though we only had two hours before bedtime, they almost always got finished with time to spare.

My kids worked faster and seemed to have an easier time if they had a break after school. I won't pretend it solved all of our homework problems, but suddenly they were more likely to grumble than to actually set their feet and refuse to work. Confrontations were fewer, and my life a whole lot simpler.

Of course, not all the difficulties caused by homework are solved this easily. At home, your student is faced with the same problems as he or she has at school. As a parent, it is hard to know how and even when to help. For the individual subjects you will find strategies to try in the chapters on math, reading and written language, but often these aren't enough. Sometimes your child will need crutches to help them along.

I know some of you are shaking your head right now and saying "I don't want my child to become dependent on a crutch." To put this into perspective, imagine that your child falls out of the neighbor's tree house this afternoon. The bone in his leg snaps and pierces the skin; it's a compound fracture! You rush him to the hospital and into surgery. With several steel pins, medical expertise, and some luck the doctor is able to piece the leg back together.

The doctor tells you everything will be fine, but your child must use crutches for six weeks. If he doesn't, his leg may not heal correctly, and he may never be able to walk normally again. I don't know a single parent who would refuse their child the use of those crutches because the child might develop a dependency. It seems stupid to even suggest such a thing, and yet there any number of parents that would deny the same kind of help for their child's academic difficulties.

As with their medical counterparts, educational crutches tend to be cumbersome and difficult to use. A child will utilize them only as long as they need to and then discard them. If a student continues using a multiplication grid or a finger to follow along in reading, it's because he still needs that crutch. Taking it away won't make him learn any faster, any more than taking away a child's crutches will make him walk better. In fact, it may do irreparable harm.

So what kinds of things can you do to help your child with homework? First you need to know exactly what kinds of activities your child has difficulty doing. Below are tasks that frequently cause students with L.D. trouble. As you go through, place a star on the line in front of those skills your child has and a minus in front of the skills your child does not have. It is a good idea to fill the checklist out with your child. You may be surprised at some of his or her answers. There may also be some that your child is not sure of. In that case, you may want to experiment a little.

Written tasks
___ Is able to write comfortably
___ Writes best with a mechanical pencil
___ Writes best with a finger grip on pencil
___ Writes best with ball-point pen
___ Is able to use a computer
___ Is able to type
___ Is able to use a spellchecker

Reading Tasks
___ Is able to gain information by reading
___ Is able to gain information by listening
___ Understands how to read textbooks for information
___ Is able to use a dictionary
___ Is able to gain understanding if he/she reads the material out loud

Mathematical Tasks
___ Knows addition/subtraction facts
___ Knows multiplication/division facts
___ Lines up numbers in math problems correctly (i.e. ones over ones in straight columns)
___ Understands story problems and is able to set up appropriate equations
___ Is able to use a calculator

Environmental concerns
___ Is able to sit still for long

periods of time
___ Likes to drink and/or eat while working
___ Needs quiet while working
___ Needs noise while working
___ Works well with music
___ Prefers bright light
___ Prefers dim light
___ Works best with long periods of uninterrupted work
___ Works best with frequent breaks
___ Needs a variety with some long periods of work and some breaks

Others

___ _____
___ _____
___ _____
___ _____
___ _____

Anything with a minus is a potential problem and everything with a star is a potential solution. For instance, if you put stars by "Works well with music", "Prefers dim light" and "Needs noise when working", you have some pretty good clues how to set up the study area.

One of the most common difficulties I've run into with my own children is the inability to write things down. Many kids with L.D. have trouble transferring coherent thoughts from their head onto paper. For many, like me, learning to type and using a computer will eventually take care of the problem. In the short run, though, written school work becomes a major dilemma. One way to solve this problem is to act as a "scribe" for your student. They dictate whatever it is they need written and you write it down for them exactly the way they say it. From there, they can either copy it into their own writing or type it.

L.D. From the Inside Out

This final step of having your child copy his work is very important. When he writes or types a word, pathways are forged in his brain. Each time the task is repeated, the pathway gets a little deeper and goes a little farther. With enough repetition, it becomes permanent. That's why it's a good idea for you to give your child a good model to copy. You will meet great resistance when you ask your child to copy what you have written down for him, but as usual there is a way around it.

In fourth grade my son Paul had to write several reports for his Wyoming History notebook. He had already written one about the ancient Indian's hunting practice of running buffalo off cliffs. Unfortunately, but not surprisingly for Paul, he'd lost it. He dictated it to me, using wonderful descriptive phrases that I guarantee wouldn't have been there had I made him write it himself. When we finished, he had a longer report than he'd originally started with and was pretty proud of himself.

Then came time to type it. At that time Paul's handwriting skills were faster than his typing. Unfortunately, even he couldn't read his writing. The paper obviously needed to be typed, but Paul was less than enthusiastic about doing it. In fact, it was clear that left to his own devices the paper would never be finished. I don't know about you, but sitting over one of my children with a club is not my favorite way to spend a Sunday afternoon. Besides, there was a show we both wanted to watch on T.V.

Perhaps it's my own L.D. but I sometimes get rather creative in my efforts to get work out of kids. That particular day I made a deal with Paul. I would type three sentences to his one. The catch was someone had to be typing at all times and we could only watch T.V. when the other person was typing. It worked like a charm, and since I attempted to coincide many of Paul's typing times with commercials, I didn't have a fight getting him to the computer on his turn.

We finished the report, proofread it and printed it out in less than an hour.[12]

All through 4th grade, Martha tried to memorize the multiplication facts. I took her through every method I knew; nothing worked. After 6 weeks of review in 5th grade, I taught her how to use a multiplication table and we moved on. With it she mastered double digit multiplication and long division. When we got to fractions the light came on. She could work problems in her head. For some reason she could look at 12 and tell you that 2/3 of it was 8, a concept most 5th graders have a great deal of trouble with. Algebra and Geometry made sense to her too. Last I heard she was taking advanced math in high school. Yes, she still has her trusty multiplication table laminated and safely tucked into the front of her notebook, but so what? With it she had the courage to tackle and master both trigonometry and calculus. If I had insisted she memorize her multiplication facts first, she'd still be working on them.

Often children with learning disabilities come up with unique methods of doing math. These should be encouraged, though you should check out their method to see if it works. My son Paul always has had a good grasp of math concepts but could never seem to memorize his facts. This caused him a great deal of trouble over the years since he always had to figure out the fact as well as the math problem he was working on. One afternoon at the beginning of sixth grade he was finishing up a math assignment in my classroom after school. Suddenly he looked us with a big grin on his face. "Hey, Mom," he said, "I just figured out what I was doing wrong with subtraction!"

"Oh really? What's that?"

"I wasn't carrying."

I'm sure I smiled. "You mean you weren't borrowing. You carry in addition and borrow in subtraction."

"No," he shook his head adamantly. "I carried."

---

[12] For more written language strategies see chapter 5

After my many years of experience with students with L.D, I knew better than to just write it down to using the wrong word, so I asked him to show me.

"Well," he said "take fifteen minus seven for instance. Seven is three away from ten so you add that onto the top number which is five and get eight. So fifteen take away seven is eight."

I was dumbfounded. How could that be? Maybe it was just a coincidence. "Try another one," I said. "How about eleven minus six?"

"Ok, six is four away from ten so add that to one and you get five. Eleven take away six is five."

We tried example after example and it worked on every one. I couldn't believe it. I still don't know why his method works; it just does. That night when he explained it to his father, my husband just grinned at me and said, "That's the way I've always subtracted."

I'm sure there are other kids out there that it would work for, but I've never shown it to my students. I'm afraid it would confuse them as badly as it did me.

Strange methods aside, a very useful tool to have handy for math homework is a calculator. Though it shouldn't be used when your child has a page of straight calculations to do, a calculator is an excellent way for students to check their own work when they are finished. Most students enjoy the sense of power it gives them to be in charge of their own corrections. It also helps them learn to use a calculator.

Calculators are also very handy when the process is the main emphasis rather than straight calculation. For instance, most story problems are intended to teach students how to use math in everyday situations. The process of setting up the problem is the main point not the actual calculation. In fact, if you're like most people, you use a calculator to check your math when you're doing something important like your checkbook or figuring out how much carpet to buy.

When you help your child with math homework, one of the most effective things you can do is check his or her work.

Put a dot by the problems that are incorrect and let your child correct them. If he is having a rough time and becoming frustrated, show him where the mistake is, emphasizing what was done correctly.

A great deal of learning takes place when a child corrects his or her mistakes. This is true of all homework. If a student makes a mistake, it stays that way in his head. When the child corrects his mistakes, he learns from it. I always tell my students that their mistakes are the best tool they have for learning.

One point of confusion I have found with parents and teachers alike, is when to help and when not to. There are times, for instance, when it's perfectly all right to read your child's textbooks to them and other times when your intervention may actually prevent the learning from taking place.

Before you begin any task with your child, stop and ask yourself what exactly it is the teacher wants the child to learn by doing it. Let's say your child has three homework assignments. The first is to read a chapter in the science book and answer questions at the end. The second is prepare for an oral report by making a recording of themselves reading a paper they have previously written. The third is to do a page of math story problems.

In the first case, the teacher obviously wants the students to understand the information in the chapter and it's perfectly ok to read it to them. Before you begin such a project it's a good idea to read the questions so your student knows what to listen for. Encourage him or her to answer the questions as you come to them in the text.[13]

The teacher's purpose in the second task was to help make the student comfortable with the written material. In this case, it is important that the student read it himself, though it is ok to help with some of the words. You might want to help your child practice a few times before he reads onto the tape.

---

[13] For more reading strategies see chapter 2

On the third task, the teacher's purpose was for the student to figure out how to set up the problem and work it. Again, for this task it is fine for you to read the problem to the child. It's not fine for you to set up the mathematical equation. What you may want to do is help him think through the problem and the solution.[14]

One word of caution here. Never under estimate your child's intelligence. Though it is tough to know exactly when to help and when not to, it's better to let your youngster struggle than to help when they don't need it. Not only can you make your student overly dependent on help, you can undercut his or her confidence. Not long after I began writing this book, a former student of mine stopped by one night after school. He stalked into the room, anger radiating from him like heat from a stove. "You know that book you're writing?" he said. "You need to tell people not to treat us like we're stupid just because we're in special ed!"

I was surprised. When George was in my class, he hadn't appeared to care much what anyone thought about him. "What happened?"

Apparently a well-meaning middle-school teacher had tried to simplify a book-report assignment for her lower functioning students. She picked four or five boys she felt would have difficulty reading a book by themselves and sent them to the library with a paraprofessional. George couldn't remember the name of the book the paraprofessional was to read to them but said it was "some stupid little kid's book".

His real beef, however, wasn't the book the teacher had chosen. His anger stemmed from the fact that he had already started a book to use for the report. It was a big thick 500 page paperback based on a popular science fiction T.V. series. He flipped to page 230 and said, "I'm already this far in it."

"Do you understand what you've read?" I asked.

---

[14] For more Math strategies see chapter 3

"Well sure," he said and proceeded to give me a detailed synopsis of what had happened in the story so far. I hadn't read the book, but he gave many details that convinced me.

"Did you tell the aide you were able to read it?"

"Yeah, but she wouldn't believe me." At that point he slapped the book down on the table. "I've read this whole book for nothing! I'm sick of people treating me like I'm stupid or something!"

I pointed out that the teacher and paraprofessional were both just trying to help and brainstormed some solutions with him. We role played a couple situations that might arise with me pretending to be the teacher. He wound up taking the book to his teacher and asking for the chance to prove once and for all that he could read it.

George was successful in more ways than one. The teacher let him do the report on his chosen book and he made an indelible impression on me as well. I, for one, will never take a student's apparent ability for granted, and now, hopefully, neither will you.

Do's and Don'ts for Homework:

* *Don't* start homework as soon as your child gets home. Set a time every night to do homework and stick to it.
* Do have a specific place for your student to do homework where he or she won't be interrupted. The kitchen table is fine as long as it isn't a focal point for the rest of the family.
* Do make sure your student has all the necessary supplies; paper, pencil, dictionary, etc. within easy access. It's not a bad idea to have a pencil sharpener near at hand.
* Do experiment with the different kinds of pencils, pens, etc. until you find the best for your child. Some students work best with long, sharp pencils, some with blunt tipped pencils and still others with little short stubs. Many students with L.D. find mechanical pencils very useful, though sometimes the distraction factor destroys any benefit.

* If your child is a snacker, provide some nutritious, high protein snacks; lunchmeat, cheese etc. Believe it or not, the brain actually likes to be fed, and protein is its favorite food.
* Do keep water handy. Brain tissues also work best if kept hydrated.
* Tape recorders and video tapes help those students unable to take notes. Most teachers have no problem with taping of their class.
* If your child is one who learns well by listening, you may want to check out the "Books on Tape" program. Created for visually impaired youngsters, it gives students with reading difficulties access to the material in their science and social studies textbooks.

I could probably write an entire book on homework helps and still not cover them all. The truth is, homework solutions, like most other topics in this book depend on the individual. You and your student will have to experiment to find what works best. Nearly every chapter in this book gives lists of strategies to try. Feel free to mix and match. As my son Paul demonstrates over and over again, there is no one right way of doing things, and your child may come up with a brand new method that will solve his homework dilemma.

Chapter 10

Chores

My mom said do the dishes,
So I suds up one or two,
Then T.V. had a movie,
That glued me to the tube.

She said to sweep the floor,
So I started with the broom,
Then my friend called on the phone,
And we talked all afternoon.

Now my mom is roaring mad,
And I just don't know why,
I did the chores she asked me to,
But she says I didn't try.
Bethany Brubaker (Teen with L.D.)

It isn't unusual for children with L.D. to have fewer chores to do than their peers or even their own brothers and sisters. It's not because they aren't capable of washing dishes or taking out the trash. It's because parents often find it easier to do it themselves than face the constant battle of getting a child with L.D. to do chores correctly. A child with L.D. frequently leaves a job half done, does it wrong, or even forgets to start it.

Imagine how frustrating it is to not remember a task long enough to finish it. Some children with learning disabilities or ADD forget what they are supposed to do before they even get started and may have to be reminded numerous times. This is not the way to make parents happy.

Take everybody's favorite, "Go clean your room." A child's idea of clean differs drastically from an adult's anyway, but for a child with a learning disability, getting her room clean may be next to impossible. When called to task, she may seem surprised that it isn't finished. Though this may be just a 'typical kid,' it may also be a product of the learning disability. Unfortunately, this is one trait that doesn't necessarily go away with age.

My own personal problem with chores is that I have a very poor short-term memory. I can't remember what I'm doing long enough to get it finished. I also have a healthy dose of ADHD along with it.

Like everything else we've discussed concerning L. D., there is usually a way to compensate for the disability. Oddly enough, I just discovered mine today, as I put this chapter together. As you read through the list below, see if you can find the key I discovered.

I got up this morning planning to clean the guest room and then get right to my writing. Since everyone else in the family was gone, I figured on sitting down at the keyboard well before noon. To get the full impact of what followed, you need to picture my house. It is a split level with the master bedroom, the guest room and the laundry room in the basement, the kitchen, living room and children's bedrooms on the second floor, and my office on the third.

* Got dressed with dog sitting there with a long face reminding me he needed to be fed. (He's lived with us for a long time and has his own way of dealing with my ADHD and poor short-term memory).

* Fed the dog and noticed a pile of laundry on my way through the laundry room.

L.D. From the Inside Out

* Decided to put in a load of laundry before starting the guest room.
* Picked up dirty clothes in my bedroom, found the liner to my daughter's snow boot.
* Set the liner on the stairs to take up to her room. Went back and made my bed. Decided my bedroom really needed to be cleaned. Started picking up, came across a broken knickknack.
* Went upstairs to my office to get the glue to fix it.
* While I was gluing the knickknack, I noticed some tapes of a conference I had ordered and decided to listen to them while I was cleaning the guest room.
* Picked up the tapes and knickknack, then went looking for the tape player. Looked in my daughter's closet. No tape player but found the snow boot so went down to get liner.
* Gathered some more laundry, remembered the liner. Put it in boot, and took it upstairs to her closet.
* Went into my son's room looking for the tape recorder. No tape recorder but noticed clothes all over his room.
* Filled his laundry basket with dirty clothes. Picked up tapes and the knickknack from the kitchen set them in the top of the laundry basket.
* Decided I'd need a cup of coffee while I was cleaning the guest room so I made a pot. While it was brewing, I decided I'd better have breakfast too. That way I wouldn't have to stop later and could get right to the guest room.
* Started making an omelet. Saw tape player sitting on table outside office. Went up stairs to get it. Finished stirring omelet and stuck it in the microwave.
* Took the tape recorder down to my bedroom with my son's laundry.
* Finally got a load of whites in and started the washing machine.
* Went back upstairs and took the omelet out of the microwave. Ate a couple of bites. Noticed the cats were hungry.

* Went upstairs to feed the cats. Found a pen I'd been looking for so I took it to the office. While I was there decided to down-load my e-mail.
* Took time to read a couple from friends. Found one that was kind of cute and decided to take it to work tomorrow. Imported it into my word processing program, fixed it up and printed it out. Stuck it in my book bag and went back down to finish my breakfast.
* Finished eating. Spent ten minutes looking for the tape player again. Found it in my bedroom. Put in first tape. Went in to get first load of clothes out of washing machine and into dryer. Put in another load.
* Got the idea for jotting this all down for the book. Sat down on the end of the bed and made notes on what I'd done so far. Started tape, dumped clean clothes on the bed, and began folding clothes.
* Finished folding clothes, then finished straightening bedroom.
* Started next load of laundry. Took clothes from the dryer back to bedroom and folded them.
* Moved tape player to guest room. Took trash out to dumpster in the alley.
* Went upstairs to get the vacuum. Warmed up coffee. Went back downstairs vacuumed bedroom.
* Cleaned downstairs bathroom
* Went back to the guest room. Started tape.
* Cleaned guest room. Made bed in guest room. Finished tape.
* Took some boxes out to dumpster. Realized lawn needed mowed.
* Went back in to put on different shoes and get my water bottle.
* Got out lawn mower. Mowed the lawn.
* Changed shoes. Fixed a sandwich for lunch.
* Took another load out of the dryer, and put one in the washing machine.
* Folded those clothes. Ate my lunch. Spent ten minutes searching for my water bottle. Took out upstairs trash.

* Found my water bottle outside on my way to the dumpster. Went back to the office and sat down at the computer. Looked at the clock. 3:00!

Frightening isn't it? Unfortunately, this is not an exaggeration; and I really *did* want to clean the guest room, believe it or not. (My sister-in-law is coming tomorrow.) Now, think of a child with the same problem. Instead of unfinished laundry, they get sidetracked by the T.V., a comic book they were reading, a video game, something going on across the street, a fight with their sister, the list is endless. Add the fact that they probably don't want to vacuum the floor in the first place, and you begin to get the picture.

Luckily, it's not hopeless. You don't have to choose between high blood pressure and doing all the chores yourself. Remember at the beginning of this chapter, I gave you the task of finding the key to helping me compensate for my distractibility? Did you find it?

When the tape was playing I stayed in the same room and did what I needed to do. Because I focused on the tape, I wasn't distracting myself with all sorts of other tasks that needed to be done. The minute the tape was off, I was running around doing six different things again. When I turned it back on again, I cleaned the guest room straight through with no side trips.

Until today, I didn't realize listening to a tape would help me. You can bet I'll be doing my housework to a tape from now on, though I may have to experiment some. A musical tape probably won't help because I can walk away without missing anything. A portable CD or tape player won't do me any good either because I could take it with me when I wander away. The key is to figure out what works and why.

So where do you start with your child? First you teach him how to do the chore. Even the simplest task may not be simple to your child. Think about when you learned to drive. Were you born knowing how to do it? Of course not. Though you had watched other people drive vehicles all your life, you had to be walked through the process several times before you ever got behind the wheel. Even then, it took months, maybe years before it became automatic for you. Your child may well need the same kind of help in learning to do their chores.

What if you've taught them how to do the task and they still can't seem to get it? Watch your children while they work. There will be things they do well. Make a list of them. Then try to figure out what makes that particular job easier and apply it to other tasks. Take a week or so to make these observations. Jot down what you discover on the lines below.

_____
_____
_____
_____
_____
_____
_____
_____
_____
_____

On the other hand, you will also see things that your child doesn't do so well, or maybe won't do at all. Try to figure out what makes it so difficult for them. Don't forget to ask your child what makes it easy or difficult. They won't always be able to tell you, but often they can at least give you an idea. Record those observations here.

_____
_____
_____
_____
_____
_____
_____
_____
_____

Once you know what they do well and what they have trouble with, you can help them figure out easier ways to get chores done. A simple solution is often easy to find and almost always best. Keep in mind, the same strategy won't necessarily work for everything. Don't be afraid to experiment with different ways of doing things. After all, you don't really care *how* it gets done as long as it does. Try not to harp. The less you say, the more likely they are to listen.

Some strategies to try
(Blanks are provided to mark ones you might like to try)
Remember this is only a starting point. You'll probably want to experiment and come up with your own solutions.

___ Do the task with them all the way through a few times. Then gradually back out until they are doing it all themselves.

___ Help your child clean his room, then take a picture. Next time, tell him to make his room look like the picture. This works for other tasks as well.

___ Break the job into small, easy-to-do tasks. "First pick up all the dirty clothes." etc.

___ Give your child one task to do at a time

___ Teach a step-by-step process of doing a particular chore.

___ Establish a routine and do it with your child several times. You may even want to make a checklist for your child to refer to.

___ Make a checklist of tasks that need to be done. OR

___ Provide a chart with tasks listed. Your child checks off steps as he finishes. Let the chart be the bad guy instead of you. (Do you have everything on your chart done?)

___ If your child seems to be wandering, ask "What's next on your chart?"

___ Write each chore on a slip of paper and put it in a box. Have the child draw one slip at a time and do the task before picking the next one. (Do this one for a break *after* the

L.D. From the Inside Out

routine is already set and your child is used to doing the chores.)

___ Set a timer and tell your child she has "x" number of minutes to complete the task.

___ Give your child a stop-watch and tell him to see how quickly that he can complete the task. (You may have to set the watch somewhere out of the way as it can become a distraction itself.)

___ Always do a particular chore at a certain time. (clean your room first thing Saturday morning- before cartoons).

___ When you give your child a task to do, have him repeat it back to you in order to make sure he understands what is expected.

___ Make a rule that work must be done before play and stick to it!

___ Say what you mean and mean what you say. (Don't give in because it is easier)

___ At regular family meetings discuss better/different ways of getting the work done.

Don't let the work or lack of it escalate into a shouting match. Go take a shower or find something else to keep yourself occupied while your children work. Once they can do it by themselves, they'll do better without you hanging over them. It makes them think you trust them to do a good job.

When my children finish a job they tell me they're ready for an inspection. I look at the job they've done, making sure I notice parts they have done well before I tell them what might need a bit more work. An inspection might go something like this. "Wow, you did a really nice job vacuuming the living room; it looks great! Would you like me to move the dining room table so you can get that spot over there?"

At times it may be tempting to give in and just do the work yourself. Resist. There is more at stake here than a tidy house or a cupboard full of clean dishes. Good work habits begin in childhood and last a lifetime. When you give your children chores and responsibilities you are teaching them skills they will need all their adult lives. By helping them discover strategies to overcome their learning disabilities you are giving them the tools they will need in the work place as well as at home. Those habits and strategies may well mean the difference between a long line of failed jobs and a successful, fulfilling career.

Praise the good work instead of focusing on what they don't have done. If you ignore the clean counter and notice only the dishes they haven't finished, next time you won't get the clean counter either. You might not love the job they did but you do love them. Be sure to tell them that and to say thank you. You'll be surprised how far, "Hey, thanks for doing the dishes. I really appreciate it," will go. Remember, the relationship with your child is more important than any lesson.

Chapter 11

Special Projects

> You must want me to lose the game,
> 'Cause you know I don't understand the rules;
> You expect me to build a castle like yours,
> But won't allow me my own tools.
> Louis R. Lampman Adult with L.D.

I have a report due next week is a phrase guaranteed to make any parent wince. For the parent of a child with L.D., it's more likely to cause cold sweats and the shakes. Though normal class work presents a difficult challenge, science projects, reports and other special projects can become nightmarish exercises in frustration. They don't have to be. By nature, students with L.D. are divergent thinkers and special projects give them a chance to shine. The trick is to figure out how to harness their natural creativity and talents while helping them around their problem areas.

My son Jason could be a poster child for ADHD (Attention Deficit Hyperactive Disorder). The words *sit still* have no meaning for him; neither does the word *quiet*. If he is surrounded by silence he makes noise, and, not surprisingly, drives his teachers nuts.

As a sixth grader, Jason wanted to participate in History Days, a statewide competition where students present projects dealing with some aspect of history. That particular year communication was the topic, and Jason chose the Pony Express as his focus.

L.D. From the Inside Out

Most participants do projects that involve elaborate poster boards and written papers. Not Jason. His particular learning disability makes reading and writing difficult for him, but he loves moving and talking. Since he isn't at all afraid of talking in front of people, he decided to do a dramatic presentation of some sort.

We went to the library and poured over books about the Pony Express. He told me what notes to write down, and figured out which pieces of information he wanted in his presentation. Somewhere along the way he got the idea of playing the part of the last Pony Express Rider as he was being interviewed by a reporter just after the final ride. With his father's help, he came up with a script, complete with questions and answers, and put together a pretty convincing costume.

With typical Jason timing, he took the final draft to school the day of the deadline. The teacher, who knew Jason as a student with L.D., was less than enthusiastic. With History Days only two weeks away, she told him he was too late.

When he came home with his chin dragging on the floor, I put in a call to the teacher and politely pointed out that Jason had met her deadline. Just as politely, she informed me Jason couldn't possibly memorize the entire script before the competition and she didn't want him to feel like a failure. It took some convincing on my part, but she finally agreed to let him try.

Reading and writing aren't Jason's bag but memorization is. He had the script memorized in two days. Not only did it meet the requirements, it was a full five minutes longer than it should have been. We cut a third of it out and he started to polish his delivery. Finally, when he was ready for his first audience, his father and I sat down to watch.

Within two minutes, we knew we had a problem. He couldn't sit still. Jason gave a flawless performance punctuated by enough excess body motion to pass for a gymnastic routine.

We had him sit backwards on the chair. He rocked back and forth, tipped the chair up on two legs and squirmed all over the seat.

We gave him two feet of rope and told him to tie knots, thinking it would keep his hands busy. It did. He swung it in circles.

We told him to hold his hat in front of him as he talked. He wadded it into a ball.

Then one of us came up with the brilliant idea for a different kind of prop. We added my grandfather's old saddle, a can of saddle soap, and a rag. As he talked to his imaginary reporter, Jason rubbed saddle soap into that old saddle. The more movement he put into it, the better the saddle looked and the more realistic his presentation appeared.

Jason took first place at the district competition and went on to state where he placed third, the highest award taken by his school. Every one of his judges gave him high marks on creativity, knowledge of his subject, and delivery. One even offered to buy the saddle.

By using his strengths, and compensating for his weaknesses, Jason put together an amazing project. His creativity and natural flamboyance won out over his learning disability and his ADHD, something I've seen happen time and time again.

If your child wants to try a special project, don't automatically assume it's beyond him. Focus on what he *can* do, and help him around things he has difficulty with. The following list of activities is designed to help you identify your child's talents. It is intended to get you started and is by no means complete. Take a few days to focus on your student's hobbies, and talents. Jot them down as you think of them. Later when your child has a special project due, use this list to generate ideas and help him plan his presentation.

What my child does well
School related activities
___reading

___writing
___penmanship
___math
___spelling
___recess-gets along with peers
___science
___social studies
___P.E.
___music
___art
___working in groups
___other school related activities
(list)

_____
_____
_____
_____

Reading/Language Arts
____ reads and understands
____ reads out loud
____ reads for fun
____ writes for fun
____ write (manuscript or cursive)
____ tells stories
____ makes up stories (verbally)
____ tells jokes
____ makes up wild tales
____ give presentations
____ writes stories
____ writes poetry
____ illustrates poems or stories
____ memorizes and/or recites poetry
____ other reading/writing activities
(list)

_____
_____

Math
___ memorizing facts
___ story problems (math reasoning)
___ addition
___ subtraction
___ multiplication
___ division
___ geometry (shapes and lines)
___ algebra
___ probability and chance
___ math puzzles
___ other math activities
(list) _____

Science
___ likes to do experiments
___ watches animal shows on T.V
___ enjoys science shows
___ likes mixing ingredients
___ interested in the weather
___ interested in the environment
___ likes science books
___ likes bugs
___ enjoys watching birds
___ enjoys tropical fish
___ interested in astronomy
___ interested in space travel
___ other science activities
(list) _____

Social Studies
____ enjoys learning about other cultures
____ likes to travel
____ plans trips
____ interested in other places
____ likes to visit old folk's homes
____ enjoys history
____ like to visit museums
____ enjoys planning parties
____ enjoys socializing
____ enjoys setting up
____ other social studies activities
(list)

_____
_____
_____
_____

Arts & Crafts
____ draws
____ cuts
____ paints
____ colors
____ draws cartoons
____ copies (pictures designs etc.)
____ makes things out of clay
____ origami (paper folding)
____ make things from paper mache
____ designs pictures, art projects etc.
____ likes to carve
____ likes wood working
____ Other
(list)

_____
_____
_____
_____

Drama
    ___ likes to play "dress-up"
    ___ likes to act out fantasies
    ___ likes to act in plays
    ___ likes to be "center stage"
    ___ likes using a dramatic voice
    ___ likes to role play
    ___ likes to pretend
    ___ likes to mimic people or characters
    ___ does impersonations
    ___ creates costumes
    ___ memorizes easily
    ___ creates 'settings' (pretend castle, island etc.)
    ___ other drama activities
(list)

_____
_____
_____
_____

Music
    ___ sings
    ___ dances
    ___ Plays a musical instrument(s) {type}
    ___ writes music
    ___ makes up songs
    ___ sings along with the radio/T.V./c.d. etc.
    ___ creates new lyrics for a song

____ other musical activities (list)

_____
_____
_____
_____

Cooking
____ cooks
____ bakes
____ decorates cakes
____ makes candies
____ tries new recipes
____ creates new recipes
____ makes breads and rolls
____ cans
____ makes jellies and jams
____ dries fruits and vegetables
____ other cooking/baking activities
(list)

_____
_____
_____
_____

Mechanics/Design/Building
____ creating lay outs
____ designing buildings, cars etc.
____ building with blocks (all types)
____ building models
____ taking things apart
____ putting them back together
____ working with wood
____ working with metal
____ enjoys working with tools
____ making paper airplanes
____ likes creating new things

___ likes electronic kits
___ other building activities
(list)

_____
_____
_____
_____

Sewing
___ sewing
___ designing clothing
___ making dolls
___ making doll clothes
___ dressing dolls
___ making crafts
___ ironing
___ crochet
___ embroidery
___ cross stitch
___ quilting
___ crewel work
___ needlepoint
___ buying/making clothes
___ modeling
___ designing a wardrobe
___ other sewing/craft activities
(list)

_____
_____
_____
_____

Sports
___ football
___ basketball
___ baseball
___ wrestling

L.D. From the Inside Out

___ soccer
___ lacrosse
___ rugby
___ hockey
___ tennis
___ badminton
___ bowling
___ golf
___ gymnastics
___ body building
___ swimming
___ running
___ pole vaulting
___ jumping
___ bowling
___ skiing
___ biking
___ racing
___ motor cycle riding
___ snow mobiling
___ roller blading
___ skateboarding
___ fishing
___ hunting
___ hiking
___ camping
___ horseback riding
___ training and/or showing animals
___ aerobics
___ weight training
___ other sporting activities
(list)

_____
_____
_____
_____

Computers
___ Computer games
___ Surfing the internet
___ figuring out new computer programs
___ creating on the computer
___ desktop publishing
___ word processing
___ creating computer graphics
___ drawing with the computer
___ Internet chatting
___ e-mail
___ other computer activities
(list)

_____
_____
_____
_____

Other skills and interests

_____
_____
_____
_____

Helping your child accentuate his or her talents sounds easy enough, but sometimes our vision of the project differs drastically from our child's. As parents, we want our children to shine. It's only natural to push them toward our way of thinking. Resist the temptation. There is no quicker way to make children lose interest or refuse to finish what they've started.

So what exactly can you help your student with? That is a difficult question since the answer varies with each project and from child to child. However, there is a simple rule of thumb to follow. If in doubt, stop and figure out exactly what the child should be learning from the project. Anything that doesn't interfere with that learning process is permissible.

In fourth grade my youngest son was involved in the Elementary Science Fair. His project dealt with bacteria and which household cleaners worked the best in killing them. Since Paul has reading and fine motor disabilities, most of my efforts were in those areas. The following two lists show a break down of the work on the project. Note, there are many things he did by himself but nothing I did alone. I only stepped in where he needed help. When the project was finished it was completely his, even down to the conclusion, which said I should clean my bathroom more than once a week!

Student with parental help

1. Helped locate sources of information
2. Identified parts of the Scientific process (I asked questions like What is your hypothesis? etc.)
3. Sterilized Petri dishes
4. Melt and pour nutrient solution
5. Bought household cleaners
6. Set up camera for "Before" shots of cultures.
7. Read directions for mixing on bottles.
8. Planned display on stand up boards.
9. Made labels for display(I did the typing)
10. Placed objects on display boards. (I helped with layout and measuring)
11. Went through several practice sessions (I was his audience/judge)
12. Packed project (I showed him how to secure his specimens)
13. Delivered student and project to school at 7:30 A.M. (All right, I confess. I did this without much help from him)

Student Alone

1. Chose project
2. Came up with "Scientific Problem" "Hypothesis" and an experiment to test his hypothesis.
3. Chose cleaners to test
4. Identified best site to grow bacteria
5. Inoculated the cultures with bacteria from his mouth.
6. Made daily observations of cultures.
7. Decided to have two "Controls" instead of one.
8. Chose the cultures to use for "Controls"
9. Took "Before" pictures of cultures.
10. Mixed solutions.
11. Added one drop to each culture.
12. Set up time table to add cleaner solutions
13. Interpreted results of experiment
14. Designed display and came up with title.
15. Dictated what he wanted typed for the display
16. Came up with presentation for judges.
17. Set up project at school
18. Won gold medal at school level, bronze at city!

Walking the fine line between *helping* and *taking over* is never easy. Often you don't even realize you've crossed that line. More than once, when I thought I was only giving my child the guidance they needed, I suddenly found myself embroiled in World War III. A blow up like that is a sure indication that you need to back off at the very least. Quite often it means you are pushing in a direction they don't want to go.

Ultimately, the project is theirs, and so are the lessons they will learn. When my daughter, Kay, took sewing in 4-H, she decided to make a flannel body pillow to show at the county fair. Everything went fine until it came time to do the final hand stitching and she ran head long into her fine motor disability. I showed her the proper method of finishing it, but Kay chose to do it her own way. It was easier and it worked. Unfortunately it didn't look particularly nice.

At our local fair, judges interview the 4-H sewing participants and often give advice on the projects. As we walked away from the building after her interview, Kay said, "You know what, Mom? My judge said I should have finished it the way you told me to."

Nothing more was said, but the next time she had hand sewing on a project she did it so that it looked nice. I suspect she learned far more by the judge telling her than if I had forced her to do it my way. As for the pillow, it was always intended as a Christmas gift for her seventeen year old brother, Jason, who loved it. He couldn't have cared less what the hand sewing looked like.

Chapter 12

The Gifted L.D.

> Sometimes I think I'm really smart,
> I soak in all I see.
> Then my teacher gives me something new,
> And my brain shuts off on me.
> *Russell Brubaker (Gifted Student with L.D.)*

Gifted L.D. may seem like a contradiction of terms until you realize how many of our gifted people had trouble in school. Thomas Edison, Eleanor Roosevelt, Winston Churchill, and perhaps the most gifted (and L.D.) of the bunch, Albert Einstein.

Gifted students with L.D. present a unique set of challenges. Rare is the school district that meets all the needs of these students. Often they won't 'qualify' for either gifted programs or special education but require both. During my career, I have taught hundreds of children with Learning Disabilities. Many were very bright and several gifted. Three, however, were exception-ally gifted.

As college students, we were assigned to various classrooms around the district to gain experience. I wound up in a junior high special ed class. That's where I met Marty. As an eighth grader Marty couldn't read, not a single word. Even 'I', 'a' and 'the' were beyond her. But she could remember everything she heard. The resource teacher taped the textbooks and Marty took all of her tests orally in the resource room.

I knew her auditory memory skills were good because I had worked with her on reports, but I had no idea how good until it came time for the standardized tests in the spring. I was to read the test to her and record her answers on the bubble sheet. After the third questions she said, "I had this test last year."

I checked the front of the test, saw that it was the proper year and the 8th grade edition. I said, "You couldn't have taken this test last year. The 7th grade test is probably very similar."

"No," she insisted. "It's the same test. I'll prove it to you." She proceeded to recite the next three test items and their answers word for word. Years later I discovered that 7th and 8th graders were given identical tests as a measure of academic growth. Marty remembered the exact wording for an entire year! I have never known another student who even realized it is the same test. Marty's incredible auditory memory was a survival mechanism created by an awesome intellect. When her text books and tests were read to her, grades went from D's and F's to A's and B's.

I had my second gifted student with L.D. several years later. Sherman was a fourth grader with minimal skills in reading and math. It was back in the days when we gave a pretest in the fall and a post test in the spring. At the end of Sherman's 5th grade year, the test put his functioning level at the middle of second grade in reading and the beginning of third in math.

It was not unusual to see a three to five month drop in scores over the summer. Sherman's generally dropped even more. When I tested him the fall of his 6th grade year, I could hardly believe my results. Suddenly, he could read at a 6th grade level and do fifth grade math! Being the curious sort, I asked him what in the world he'd done over the summer that had improved his reading and math so much.

"Well," he said, "a new boy named Steve moved in next door, and he gave me some really neat books to read. Have you ever heard of J.R. Tolkien and the Lord of the Rings trilogy? They're the best books in the world!"

For those of you who have never actually read *The Lord of the Rings,* it is a very complex story full of all sorts of odd characters with strange names. It's challenging for adults yet Sherman jumped into it with second grade reading skills and understood it! No wonder his reading scores went up.

"That explains reading," I said, "but J. R. Tolkien didn't teach you how to multiply."

His eyes lit up. "No, I got that from a game Steve taught me. It's called Dungeons and Dragons."

By the time Sherman had finished explaining the game, which I had never heard of at the time, he'd gone so far over my head I felt like I was drowning. Needless to say, Sherman was out of special ed. soon after that. I'd like to say I had something to do with his amazing academic growth, but truthfully the credit goes to J.R. Tolkien and Dungeons and Dragons.

My third gifted student was David. Like Marty and Sherman, David had trouble pretty much across the board, but reading was his nemesis. The first indication that he might be a tad bit different than most kids came when he asked if he could see his special ed file. I'd never had such a request, neither had our school diagnostician. In fact, the *law* didn't even address it. We decided it fell under the same ruling as a parent's right to see anything in the files and set up an appointment for David to visit with the diagnostician.

David listened very carefully as she explained all the tests and his scores. Then he asked some incredibly astute questions. At the end he nodded with great satisfaction. "There," he said, "I *knew* I was Dyslexic!" Frankly, I never saw another fifth grader who even knew what Dyslexia was, let alone what kind of test scores to look for. It's not an educational term and certainly wasn't in his records anywhere.

David's high level of intelligence became even more obvious as time went on. When our class won first prize in a school contest, we became the proud owners of a magnificent dragon kite. The afternoon we took it out and flew it all the kids fell in love, especially David. The question arose about who would get our wondrous kite at the end of the year. I finally came up with the idea of using the "bonus bucks" the students earned for their work and used to buy things like gum passes and new pencils. Whoever had the most bonus bucks at the end of the year went home with the kite.

Because David spent most of his time with other teachers, he was way behind in the bonus buck department. He immediately set out to even the odds. First he pointed out how much fun it might be to have an auction. When I agreed, he encouraged the other kids and even other teachers to bring things from home to add to it. As our auction grew, so did the kids' excitement. Pretty soon the kite became one of many irresistible selections.

One Friday afternoon in late spring David casually suggested I give them an extra recess as a reward for a week of hard work. Within a few minutes he had the other kids whipped into a frenzy of pleading. When I failed to fall in with their plan, David said. "Ah come on, Mrs. Bru, we'll each pay you a bonus buck if you'll let us go outside. Shucks we'll even pay you *five* bonus bucks, won't we guys?"

They almost deafened me with their eager response. I knew I wouldn't get another ounce of work out of them anyway, so I agreed to the extra recess. The kids gleefully handed me their bonus bucks and headed for the playground, all of them except David. As the others trooped outside, he went back to his seat and calmly picked up his pencil.

"David," I said, "aren't you going out for recess?"

"Nope. I've got work to finish."

"But you just spent all that time talking me in to an extra recess! All the others are outside."

He flashed me a grin. "Yeah, and they each paid you five bonus bucks to do it. I'm that much closer to getting the kite!"

When the auction finally arrived, it looked as though all David's hard work was going to pay off. It boiled down to David and a developmentally delayed girl I had in class. Though Sally had already 'purchased' several things, she still had a pretty good bank roll. David hadn't even bid on anything else and I knew he had one more than she did.

The bidding was hot and heavy between them; they both wanted that kite, bad. I'm still not sure why, but at the last minute David stepped back and let Sally have the high bid. Sally was thrilled. She didn't have a clue what he'd done, but I sure did. David walked out of that classroom with a pocket full of worthless bonus bucks and a big smile on his face. He's been my hero ever since.

Gifted students with L.D. are sometimes called twice exceptional. Marty, Sherman, and David are extreme examples, but they prove a point. The most skeptical teacher would have little trouble seeing Marty, Sherman and David as very bright students, even if they didn't accept the gifted diagnosis.

Others are gifted in other areas such as music, art, drama, writing, athletics etc. They are even easier to spot. One of my brothers is a gifted poet. Another can design and build anything you want out of wood or metal. Both struggled in school especially the artistic one. Often, the very students that have classroom teachers pulling their hair out are the same students that the art, music or PE teachers love to have in class.

Not all twice exceptional students are obvious, however. Often the high intelligence and the learning disability mask each other. That isn't necessarily bad; such students usually manage to function in the classroom. However, they may never reach their full potential because no one realizes how very bright they are. In my experience, the more intelligent the child is, the more severe their learning disability seems to be. A student as bright as Marty, for instance, would probably be able to compensate for a mild to moderate learning disability without anyone being the wiser.

L.D. From the Inside Out

As a high school student, my husband was always steered away from higher-level math and science. He never attempted algebra, trigonometry, physics, or chemistry. In fact, those were the very classes he should have been in. He taught himself the basics of trigonometry and figured out surveying pretty much on his own. When he finally took physics in college ten years later, he aced it. Think what he might have been able to do if he'd been allowed to take those classes as a teenager. It may well have changed his life!

Twice exceptional students are usually able to absorb great quantities of knowledge. They have come to accept it as natural and are used to learning quite easily. Everything is fine until they enter school and suddenly come up against their learning disability. It's like slamming into a brick wall.

Take my youngest son, a gifted child with a reading/language disability. Before he even got to school, Paul knew the names and habitats of most of the world's animals, understood gravity well enough to explain it, and had a working knowledge of aerodynamics. By the time he reached fourth grade, he was ready to explore chemistry, physics and astronomy. At the same time, the books he could read were created for second and third graders. He saw them as boring and silly. Even the few based on science were too simplistic to be of any interest to him. The books he *wanted* to read were several years beyond his grade level and miles beyond his own reading ability.

Paul is not unique. Most twice exceptional students experience similar gaps. The result is a growing sense of frustration that can erupt in inappropriate ways. These students are often characterized as lazy, off-task, careless or belligerent troublemakers.

How do you know if your child is twice exceptional, and what do you do about it? Those are excellent questions. Unfortunately, there is no easy answer for either. The following list contains some signs that may indicate high intelligence.

___Uses lots of large or colorful words when they speak
___Has a vivid imagination
___Looks at things differently
___Can see both sides of a debate
___Finds their own way of solving problems; often comes up with unusual solutions
___Is very creative
___Often has insights that seem way beyond their years
___Has well developed sense of right and wrong
___Has an advanced sense of humor; understands jokes and plays on words other kids their age don't
___Wants to read books about subjects far more advance than is "normal" (reading skills maybe considerably lower)
___Enjoys documentaries on television
___Fixates on a certain subject, dinosaurs for example, and wants to know everything there is to know about it. For weeks they eat, sleep, and breathe "dinosaurs"
___Comes up with elaborate games of "let's pretend"
___Enjoys museums and other "educational" activities
___Is perfectly content to spend time alone working on "projects"
___Likes to experiment.
___Asks lots of "what if" questions.
___Has "strange" ways of doing school work that get the right answers but make little sense to

anyone else.
___Always seems to be a step ahead
___Likes to take things apart to see how they work
___Prefers "building" toys to "user" toys
___Enjoys games of strategy
___Has one or more 'collections'

There are several ways you as a parent can provide the enrichment twice-exceptional children need. Look for books in their interest area that have lots of pictures with good captions. Take family field trips to museums, the library etc. Volunteer to read books and articles on subjects that interest your children but are above their reading levels. Provide the proper tools for hobbies that interest them. Encourage them to explore new interests.

The following are some activities your child might like to try. It doesn't matter if they are gifted or not; these activities appeal to a wide variety of children. If you don't find anything they particularly enjoy among these, branch out. These are merely a starting point. Look for activities that stimulate the mind, and encourage creative thinking. There are many games on the market, computer and otherwise, that stimulate learning.

- Mind stretchers (or benders)
- Games of strategy
- Games that stress vocabulary
- Games that deal with knowledge of trivia
- Chess
- Backgammon
- Word finds and other word puzzles
- Computer adventure games that involve collecting or following clues to solve a puzzle.

- Computer simulations games
- Extra curricular activities- 4-H, scouting etc.
- Inventor or building competitions
- Entering contests
- Community Theater
- Community college classes
- Athletics
- Young Authors or other writing contests
- Science discovery kits
- Art supplies
- Explore a variety of crafts
- Writing/telling stories
- Desktop publishing
- Supervised exploration of the Internet

You may be wondering what happened to my three "gifted" students. Marty owns and operates a very successful business. Her spouse does the books and takes care of all correspondence leaving Marty free to use her creative genius. Sherman graduated in the top one fourth of his class and is now a building contractor. While still in High School, David's Odyssey of the Mind team placed in the top three in three international competitions. He is considerably younger than the other two and only recently graduated from high school. Currently, he is going to college and majoring in pre-med. I can hardly wait to see what heights he will rise to.

Chapter 13

Preparing Yourself for the IEP Meeting

> To you he is an irritant,
> The one who wrecks your day.
> To me he is a precious gift,
> Worth more than I can say.
>
> He's not just a bunch of numbers,
> Or a problem in your class.
> The testing won't define him,
> And your labels will not last.
>
> He isn't stupid, dull or dumb,
> Though he may seem that way,
> You can not see inside his head,
> Where his awesome powers lay.
>
> As you decide his future,
> With your Child Study Team,
> Remember he is my whole life,
> And the focus of my dreams.
> *Carolyn Brubaker*
> *Mother of four children with L.D.*

Warning: You are about to enter the world of educational techno-babble! The special education system loves to give everything long technical names then shorten them to a set of initials. The vocabulary is filled with terms like STO, LRE, BIT, MDT, and IEP. Even the federal law that regulates special education is known as IDEA (Individual with Disabilities Education Act). Unfortunately, educators are so used to using these terms that they often forget that parents don't always understand all the jargon that gets thrown around at meetings. To make maters even worse, there is no universal language. Terms differ from state to state and from district to district.

The purpose of this chapter is to acquaint you with the special education process and all those confusing terms. To make this chapter usable, I have provided a thumbnail glossary of the terms you will encounter. Skim through it now, then read the chapter. If you run into something you don't understand, flip back to the glossary. Keep in mind that any of these may be called something else in your district or state. The process will still be much the same, however, and you will soon be able to substitute the appropriate terms for what I have used here.

BIT- Building Intervention Team or screening committee

Case manager- the person in charge of all the paperwork involved with a particular child

Child Study- an IEP meeting

IDEA- Individuals with Disabilities Education Act (Public Law 105-17)

IEP- Individual Educational Plan- the individualized plan to educate your child

IEP meeting- A meeting at which an IEP is developed

Inclusion- Special education services delivered in the regular classroom

Initial evaluation- The first set of testing done

IQ- a measure of intellectual ability

LRE- Least restrictive environment

Pullout- Special education services delivered outside the regular classroom

Separate Class- A special education placement where the special ed classroom is the student's home base- usually the most restrictive placement provided within a school district.

Referral- When the special education staff is asked to test a child for possible placement

Resource room- a special education placement outside the regular classroom usually for one or two periods per day

Service Provider- A teacher or other professional who works with a student on an IEP

Services- Assistance a student on an IEP receives.

STO- Short term objectives- skills the service providers will work on with the student.

Support- Special education services delivered outside the regular classroom that supplement instruction in the regular classroom.

Replacement- Special education services delivered outside the regular classroom that replace instruction in the regular classroom

As this book goes to press, the special education law is in the process of being rewritten. Until the new law goes into effect, state departments and school districts across the nation operate under public Law 105-17. Called Individuals with Disabilities Education Act or *IDEA*, this law covers the education of all handicapped students. [15] The next two chapters deal with the portion of the law pertinent to students with learning disabilities as the law now stands. It is recommended that you check with your state department for the current special education laws.

By law, every student placed in Special Education must first have an evaluation. The purpose of the evaluation is to determine if the child has a disability and to help design a program of instruction for that child. Each child who is identified with a disability has an Individual Education Plan or IEP. Each IEP is unique and is specifically tailored to help that

---

[15] You can obtain a copy of the IDEA law from your State Department of Education or read it in its entirety at www.Ed.gov/offices/OSERS/IDEA/the_law.html

student learn the same information and skills as his or her peers in the regular classroom.

It is vitally important that you become involved in the IEP process. Though school personnel have their students' best interests at heart, they can't possibly know your child the way you do. You and the school share the education of your student and a strong positive relationship between you can only benefit your child. One of the most important things you can do is keep the lines of communications open. The more involved you are, the more likely you are to be satisfied with the program eventually set up for your child.

The IEP meeting is often the parent's first real experience with the special education process. Every child placed in Special Education must first go through a battery of tests given by a team of 'experts'. Then the team meets with the parents and the classroom teacher in an IEP meeting, or Child Study Meeting as it is sometimes known. If the child 'qualifies', the IEP committee creates an Individual Education Plan (known as IEP) that outlines what kinds of services the student will receive, who will be providing those services and even what objectives the student will work on.

The way the federal law is written, a child's handicapping condition must be identified before a child can receive special education services. Each recognized "handicap" has a specific set of criteria that must be met. The criteria for L.D. differ from state to state. You can find out what your own state's requirements are by contacting your state department of education or your local special education director.

Many states use what is called a discrepancy model to define an L.D. handicap. Using this model, there has to be a big gap between what the I.Q. test says a child should be able to do and what the achievement test says he is doing. It's a numbers game. In my home state, for instance, there has to be a 22-point discrepancy. That means if the child has an IQ of 100, he/ she must score a 78 or below to qualify for special education.

Let's say Johnny, a fourth grader, has an IQ of 100 and his achievement scores are math 76, reading 82, and written language 79. In terms of grade placement, his skills would all be in the late second or early third grade range. Even though he is obviously way behind in all academics, Johnny would qualify for special education in math but not written language and reading. In some states, however, if he qualified for L.D. in any category, he could receive services for anything he needed. In Johnny's case, that would mean all three: math, reading and written language. It is very important for you to be aware of what rules and regulations exist in your state.

According to federal law, parents must be included in the IEP process, but as a parent I've found it very easy to get railroaded into an IEP that didn't meet my child's needs. Your best protection is knowledge. The process is long and complex. Though it is frustrating for both parents and teachers, it was created to prevent children from being incorrectly labeled. When you consider how a label might affect a child's future, you begin to realize why getting the right one is so important. If you know how the process works and what your child's rights are, you will be in a far better position to help the professionals develop the best IEP for your child. It is a team effort and you'll want to be an active, contributing member of that team.

Like criteria for handicapping conditions, exact procedures differ from state to state and even from school district to school district. However, since it is mandated by the federal government, the process is fairly similar everywhere. To get a clear picture of what happens, let's follow a child through. Keep in mind your district may do things somewhat differently.

The process begins with a teacher or parent noticing the child starting to flounder. If you, as a parent, request that your child be tested for a disability, the school district is under no obligation to do so if they feel there is no reason to test your child. If you truly feel your child has a handicap and are unable to get the school district to evaluate your child, you do have options available to you. These are described at length in Chapter 14.

Typically, when a child begins to have difficulty in school, the teacher will dig into her bag of tricks and try a variety of strategies. In the meantime, to get a clearer picture of what is going on, the teacher may also pull the child's cumulative file to see how he or she has done on the standardized tests in prior years, talk to previous teachers, and contact the child's parents.

If it appears to be an ongoing problem, the teacher proceeds to the next step which is generally the Building Intervention Team or some type of school screening committee. The BIT is a team of professionals that usually includes several teachers and the building principal. It is the BIT's job to review existing information and determine if an evaluation is necessary. They will look at test scores on standardized tests, review the documentation, both current and from years past. As part of this step, they talk to the child's teacher. Most experienced teachers will have already tried many different interventions, and the BIT will try to suggest others like one-on-one work with a para-educator, or perhaps a different teaching method.

The teacher tries those suggestions for a period of time after which the BIT reconvenes. As a team, they review the documentation and decide if the student should be referred for testing. This step is not mandated in all states, but most school districts have some sort of screening procedure in place.

From the BIT, the case is turned over to Special Education and a case manager is assigned. The case manager is the paper pusher in charge of the case. It is their job to review the information and documentation gathered by the BIT or referring teacher, set up an initial evaluation, gather reports and information, and compile all the data in preparation for the IEP meeting.

Before the referral goes any further, you will be asked to sign permission to test. Once you have given your permission, the evaluation process will begin.

The law states that a child may *not* be placed in special education on the basis of one procedure or test. Make sure your child is being tested in all areas of concern. The actual tests are given by a multiple disciplinary (MDT) team of professionals, many of whom may later be working with your child. A speech therapist might be responsible for speech/language testing, for instance, a special education teacher for academics, and the occupational therapist for fine motor/handwriting testing. The team will give the tests and lend their expertise in deciding whether special services are called for. They may also help develop the IEP. The tests given depend on the child and his or her needs.

Generally an intelligence test is assigned to establish a child's learning potential, or IQ, and academic testing is done to determine their math, reading and written language levels. Many districts also routinely give oral language assessments, as learning problems are often related to a child's inability to understand or process spoken language.

Several other kinds of tests may be given depending on what difficulties that child is experiencing in school. An occupational therapist might be asked to evaluate fine motor or handwriting skills, a physical therapist to test coordination, or an audiologist to assess hearing and processing. If the BIT identifies behavioral or psychological concerns, a psychological evaluation may also be done. Again, the types of tests given vary from district to district. Often districts are as receptive to parent requests as those of teachers. So if there is some test you or the teacher feel would be beneficial, it doesn't hurt to ask for it. Your request may be denied, but you'll never know until you try.

In addition to testing, a variety of other information is gathered. Vision and hearing screenings are usually done to rule out problems in those areas. Various individuals will make classroom observations to see how the child functions in the classroom, and how he or she adapts to change. The school social worker may have all of the child's teachers fill out a behavior checklist in order to determine if the same problems exist in all settings.

As a parent, you will probably be interviewed or asked to fill out an extensive questionnaire to build a complete case history. Though some of the questions may be difficult to answer or even seem a bit intrusive, the information is vital if the team is to develop a complete picture of your child. Some learning disabilities can be traced from early childhood, and learning patterns begin long before a child starts school. You may be asked when they began to sit up, crawl, walk, and talk, or if there have been any health problems like high fevers.

Frankly, by the time my kids were in school and having difficulties, I had trouble remembering exactly when those all important events took place. Their baby books turned out to be a life-saver. If you don't have a similar source and can't recall the exact dates, do the best you can.

You will also be asked about your child's school experiences, abilities, needs and his/ her behavior outside of the school setting. There may be important information that isn't covered in the interview. Any family situation that is causing stress in the child's life is significant. A death in the family, a new baby, a divorce, or a move can all have a major impact. Make sure the school knows about any illness or conditions that exist such as Rheumatoid arthritis, seizures, asthma, or allergies. Even if your child no longer has the condition, it is important for the school personnel to know. You should also list *any* medication, including those for allergies. The more information the professionals have, the more complete picture they will get of your child.

Finally, after all the tests are given and the information gathered, an IEP meeting will be set up. The IEP meeting is the most important part of the process because it may change your child's education dramatically. As a parent, you want to make sure the changes are the best possible choice for your child.

What exactly is the IEP meeting? The purpose of the IEP meeting is to determine if your child is eligible for special education services and to write an IEP (Individual Educational Plan) if one is needed. The parents, the regular classroom teacher, an administrator, someone who can interpret the test results, those who gave tests and everyone who may be working with your child are invited to attend. These people make up the IEP or Child Study Committee. You are a vital part of this committee. In fact, the IEP meeting must be scheduled at a time when you are able to attend, and no change in placement can be made without your permission. If you are unable to attend, the school may hold the meeting without you. They must, however, keep you informed of what is happening.

To prepare for the meeting you may want to make a list of your child's strengths and weaknesses. If there is a chance your child will be placed in a special education classroom, you might want to visit the classroom before hand and talk with the teacher. You may also want to discuss what is happening with your child.

It's not a bad idea to take along a paper and pencil for taking notes. So much information will be presented to you that you may well have a difficult time processing and understanding all you hear. If taking notes is too distracting for you, you may want to take a tape recorder instead. I find this especially useful if my husband is unable to attend the meeting with me since I tend to forget all the little details. As a courtesy, you should explain that you will be taping and why before the meeting starts.

It is a good idea for both parents to attend whenever possible. You are also welcome to take anyone you wish to the meeting. Though they will not actually be part of the IEP committee, it's sometimes nice to have someone along for moral support.

Once everyone at the meeting has been introduced, you will be given a copy of your rights and they will be explained to you. [16] Then the meeting gets down to business. First the

---

[16] A copy of parental rights (procedural safe guards) is available in Appendix 1

team decides eligibility. Everyone who gave tests will present their findings. You may request copies of their reports for your files if you wish. The IEP committee will discuss possible handicapping conditions. This is where your child would be labeled as learning disabled.

Once the handicapping condition has been identified, an individual educational plan (or IEP) is developed. The purpose of an IEP is to set reasonable goals for your child and to state the services (assistance) the school will provide. This plan outlines how much time will be spent in each service, the objectives that each service provider will focus on, and what the expected outcomes are. Typically, a child might receive math and reading from the resource teacher, oral language therapy from the speech therapist, and fine motor training from the occupational therapist. The services your child receives will depend on what needs were identified by the testing.

The IEP is a legal document and, by law, must be created at the meeting. However, to save time, the school personnel will often bring proposed goals and objectives or even a sketched out IEP to the meeting. Keep in mind, it is not carved in stone and can be changed. If there is something you feel your child should receive but isn't suggested, don't be afraid to bring it up. School personnel usually welcome parental input.

Each service provider will present you with proposed goals and objectives. A goal is the outcome you would eventually like to see. It usually covers a large area. For instance a goal for math might be: *Student effectively applies mathematical principles and operations to solve a range of math-ematical problems.* Short term objectives are the steps that it will take to meet the goal. For instance, a math objective under the preceding goal might be *"Given 30 addition facts to 10, the student will give the correct answers with at least 90% accuracy two out of three times."* Each should include the accuracy level or a criteria and a statement of how the goal will be evaluated. Teacher charting, or daily work samples are often used as methods of documentation.

Many parents want to know when a certain goal or objective will be met. Service providers usually won't give you a date because they don't know. Children learn at different rates and in many different ways. It may take the teacher awhile to find out which method is the most effective and even then it won't be possible to predict just when a student will meet a particular goal. A better question might be to ask what the final expectation is and what the next step might be once that objective is met.

IEP goals and objectives should reflect the school district standards and benchmarks as much as possible. Even though your child may need to be taught at a different rate, she will need to learn the same skills as her peers. Not only will she be held to the same graduation standards as her peers, many students with learning disabilities eventually work their way out of special ed and back into the mainstream fulltime. As a parent you'll want this transition to go as smoothly as possible.

Another important aspect of the IEP meeting is placement. According to the law, the child must be placed in the Least Restrictive Environment (or LRE). The least restrictive environment simply means the setting with the least amount of intervention needed for your child to receive an appropriate education. In other words, she can't be placed in a pull-out special education setting if extra help in the classroom will do the trick.

There are several types of resource environments for students with L.D. offered by school districts. The least restrictive is the *inclusion setting*. Inclusion means the child stays in the regular classroom with some support from special education in the form of a teacher or para-professional. Sometimes that extra help is all a child needs to function in the regular classroom. The philosophy of inclusion is that students who stay with their classmates are more accepted by their peers as well as being exposed to the same learning as the rest. The down side is that most school districts can't afford a fulltime special ed teacher or aide in each classroom, so for most of the day the students are on their own. There is also little chance for students to "catch up" on concepts they've missed in the past.

A *pull-out* program is one that pulls the student from the main classroom for a certain part of the day. The regular classroom is their home base, but they go to a resource room and work with the special education teacher in the subjects that cause them problems. Depending on your child's needs, this can either be for *support* or *replacement.*

A *support* program is one that provides additional instruction or practice on whatever concept is being taught in the regular classroom. For example, your child might get an extra half an hour of reading or extra help on a math concept the class is working on. For the program to be really successful the two teachers need to work together. It makes no sense, for instance, for a child to be working on addition in the resource room and multiplication in the regular classroom. If your child takes a little longer to grasp new concepts but can usually keep up with some additional instruction, support will probably be quite effective for him or her.

A *replacement* program is one that takes the place of the regular classroom instruction. If a child is two years behind in a subject it makes little sense to leave the child in the regular classroom for instruction. With a replacement program the resource teacher can start where the child is and teach from there. Though it may seem that the child would never catch up, my experience has been just the opposite. By taking a student back to a level at where they can experience success, I have found they gain confidence and momentum. I have had many students who catch up with their peers in a few years and no longer need services.

On the positive side, unlike inclusion, in a pull-out program the child can move at his own pace. Often they learn concepts they missed and are suddenly able to understand other more difficult material. The down side of pull-out is that the child is no longer part of the mainstream classroom for that subject. In some cases their classmates do get farther and farther ahead.

The third type of placement is a *separate classroom*. It is just what it sounds like. The special ed classroom becomes the child's home base and he goes out for what he can handle with his grade-level peers. For instance, a child might have math, reading and language in the special ed classroom but go to regular ed for art, music, P.E., and social studies. This placement is the most restrictive offered by most districts. Though there are some residential schools dedicated entirely to students with learning disabilities, most are private.

Your school district may not have all the programs I've just described. It is very difficult, for instance, to have an inclusion program and pull-out in the same school unless there is more than one resource teacher. Chances are, the IEP team will recommend the placement that is best for your child. However, it is a good idea to be aware of what programs are available in your district. Don't be afraid to ask questions.

As soon as placement has been determined and goals and objectives proposed, the amount of time your child will actually spend in special ed will be decided. This includes all special education classes and any other related services like speech therapy or adaptive P.E. Each will have its own set of goals and objectives which will be proposed to you.

There will also be a discussion of appropriate accommodation to be used during district-wide or standardized tests. Since the purpose of such tests is to find out how much the student knows, every attempt is made to insure the results are an accurate measure of that knowledge. If a child with a reading disability has to read the social studies test, the results will probably show how well they could read the questions, not how much he or she knows about social studies. Similarly, a student with a fine motor disability or a visual tracking problem might not be able to color in the bubbles on the answer sheet accurately. Accommodations might be having directions and test items read aloud, or a scribe to transfer answers to the bubble answer sheet.

Modifications and accommodations allowed differ somewhat from state to state and from test to test, but you can get a list from your local special education director. Once in place, these accommodations may be used for any test situation including classroom tests.

Finally, you will be asked to sign the IEP. It is important to keep in mind that an IEP is a legal document. You should give it as much consideration as you would any other contract you sign. If you aren't comfortable with something, negotiate it now. Once an IEP goes into affect, the school is bound by law to follow it exactly. If you feel you need to think about it over night, *don't sign*! It is very difficult to change an IEP once it is in place.

Once you have signed it, the IEP will go into effect and services will begin. According to the current law, an IEP must be reviewed at least once a year. Usually this takes place in an annual review. The annual review is much like the initial placement IEP meeting except there usually hasn't been any additional testing. The regular classroom teacher will be there to give a full report on how your child is progressing in the regular classroom. In addition, each teacher or service provider who has worked with your child will review their objectives and propose new ones. A new IEP will be developed the same way the last one was.

Objectives, goals, or placement cannot be changed without another meeting. If a change becomes necessary between annual reviews, an *interim meeting* is called. Say little Johnny has met all his speech goals but still needs the help he gets in the resource room. An interim meeting would be called to release him from speech.

Every three years the school district will conduct a re-evaluation. This is the same basic process as the first evaluation. If there is some area you feel needs to be tested, feel free to suggest it. Once the testing is finished, a new label will be determined and a new IEP written. Though the IEP is a legal document, it is not a contract. The school must make a good-faith effort to help the student meet their goals and objectives. However, if your child fails to meet the goals and objectives, the school can not be held responsible. If you feel your child is not progressing, you may want to contact the school and request an interim review to revise the IEP. If, for some reason, a problem arises that cannot be worked out, you have the right to ask for a due process hearing, which is discussed at length in the next chapter.

There are certain things that by law need to be on the IEP. Below is a handy checklist to take to the meeting with you. Make a copy and check off each as it comes up. If there is anything left out or that you have a question about, bring it up.

Does the IEP include:

___ A statement of the child's present level of performance

___ Special education and related services your child will receive.

___ Measurable annual goals

___ Short term objectives (or bench-marks)

___ A statement of how the goals and objectives will be evaluated

___ Dates when services will begin and end

___ A statement of the length of time your child will spend in each service

___ The time in special education verses the time in regular education

___ A statement about the strengths of the child

___ A statement about the concerns of the parent

___ The results of the initial or most recent evaluation of the child

___ Results of most recent state or local standardized testing

___ A statement detailing how often parents will be notified of progress on goals and objectives. This should be as often as you are informed of progress in the regular classroom. In my district it's every nine weeks when report cards come out

___ A statement about related

services (speech therapy, counseling etc.) and/ or supplementary aides if appropriate. Most of these services will also have goals and objectives.

___ Accommodations and modification for national, state, and/or district assessments

___ An explanation of the extent, if any, to which the child will not participate with non-disabled students in the regular class.

___ A statement about behavior con-cerns. (Is a behavior plan other than the school's regular discipline plan needed for this child?)

___ Were you given a copy of your rights?

___ Did you and everyone else at the meeting sign the IEP?

___ Were you given a copy of the IEP? (This may be mailed to you later. If you don't get a copy, be sure to ask.)

___ Were you given a copy of all test reports that you requested?

Chapter 14

When Parents and School Disagree

Avoid litigation. Compromise when you can.
Abraham Lincoln

In a perfect world there would be no need for this chapter. Parents and school personnel would always see the child the same way. Everyone would agree on the path the student's education should take, and there would never be a difference of opinion.

, the world is not perfect and disagreements do occur. Usually, school districts and parents are able to work out a solution that both sides find acceptable. When this isn't possible, the law makes provisions for parents to challenge the school district, or in some cases, for the school to challenge the parents. Due Process is a legal safety net set up for the child when parents and school don't agree. Whenever a request is made for a Due Process hearing, the student's placement does not change until the disagreement can be settled. It is intended to provide consistent services for the child no matter how intense the dispute.

As a parent and a teacher, I have been on both sides of the table. Though it isn't always possible, compromise is the best alternative. If things get ugly, and they can, your child is stuck right in the middle. One of the most difficult things I've ever had to do as a parent was send my son back to school the day after a meeting with teachers and the principal turned into a shouting match.

Every district has its own interpretation of the law and its own policies, making it impossible to discuss every scenario that can arise. They are as many and varied as the students, families, and schools involved. So are the solutions. Still, there is a right and wrong way to do things, both from the parents' perspective and from the schools' perspective. It isn't always easy to decide the best way to go.

At my son Paul's annual review in fifth grade, the child study committee discussed what kinds of accommodations he would need in sixth grade. Our middle school consists of 6th, 7th, and 8th grade. We all felt Paul could handle everything in the regular classroom as long as he had support to help him organize and keep up with his work.

At the time of our meeting, a special ed support class was available at the middle school. It was a glorified study hall where students could finish work under the watchful eye of the resource teacher. This teacher was in contact with classroom teachers and was able to keep track of work that needed to be done, classes students were having trouble with, and up-coming projects. The child-study team felt that with a support class Paul would be able to function just fine in the middle school and wrote the IEP to reflect that.

That spring the middle school decided to change to a block schedule. Because of scheduling problems, the support class was axed. Most of the resource kids were placed on the same team and a special ed paraprofessional was provided in each class to help them. Teachers and administrators felt this solution would better meet the needs of the population with L.D.

The first I knew of the change came in a letter shortly after the beginning of school. It explained the change and said Paul's IEP had been modified as a result. It went on to say that if the school district had not heard from me by September 15, they would assume I was in agreement.

I immediately wrote a letter explaining why the child-study committee had recommended the support class and expressing concern for the coming year. The next day, I received a visit from the case manager. We both explained where we were coming from and agreed that an interim meeting was necessary to set up a new program.

I took Paul to the meeting with me since I knew nothing would work if he didn't buy into it. It was a very congenial meeting. Teachers discussed what sorts of things would be expected of Paul. In turn, he and I explained what activities caused him problems and what had worked for him in the past. As a committee, we came up with several possible solutions including having someone check his daily planner and letting him dictate stories and reports to the special ed paraprofessional. Since his annual review date was in early October, I suggested we change it until after the end of the first nine weeks so we'd be able to judge the results of the new program.

At the end of the first nine weeks, we reconvened. I commented on how pleased we'd been with Paul's report card, all A's and B's. The case manager said, "Do you have any idea how much support it took for him to accomplish that?"

I just smiled and replied, "So, now do you understand why we put him in a support class?"

The meeting turned into a brainstorming session as we worked together to create a workable IEP. We kept the portions of the previous plan that had been successful and discarded those that hadn't. To tie home and school together, we added a weekly communication from the teachers that came to us through the mail. Every teacher gave Paul's current grade and wrote down any assignments he was missing. For each class that was marked ok, he earned time on Saturday to play his favorite computer game.

Since it was obvious that Paul really did need a supervised study hall, we explored all the possibilities for giving him one. Though they no longer had a special ed study hall, there was one for students who were missing assignments after school each day. Paul became a permanent member. It wasn't a perfect solution; his day was a full hour and a half longer than his peers, and he couldn't participate in extra-curricular activities. It did, however, keep him caught up with his homework and alerted us to any problem areas before they turned into major issues. By parents and school personnel working together, we created a win/win situation. Paul got the help he needed and teachers got work handed in on time.

The school and the parents working as a team for the child's benefit is always the best case scenario. Unfortunately it isn't always possible. When my older son, Jason, was in middle school we faced a similar problem in another school district. The process and ultimate results were very different.

Though Jason had problems all the way through school, he wasn't actually placed in the resource room until 4th grade. At the time his 'label' was emotionally disturbed, though the psychologist and a medical doctor had both diagnosed ADHD. About the same time a shake up in the school district had resulted in a new administration and an entirely new special ed staff.

We clashed with the new staff almost immediately, and there were skirmishes every time we went to a meeting. I drove home from a child-study meeting in tears more than once, and I'm sure the special ed department hated to see me coming. Still, we managed to put appropriate IEP's together and an uneasy truce existed between home and school.

When Jason's three year re-evaluation came up in sixth grade, the psychologist's report stated that though Jason still exhibited some symptoms of emotional disturbance, his primary handicap was Attention Deficit Hyperactive Disorder.

Jason was taking Ritalin and the difference was astounding. Within twenty minutes of Jason taking his medication, his father and I could see a difference. Yet, for some reason, the ADHD diagnosis didn't sit right with the school, and they refused to acknowledge it. I pushed for a change in label but was pretty much ignored. The school had brought every teacher that had anything to do with Jason to the Child Study meeting. At thirteen to one I was clearly outnumbered, outvoted and more than a little intimidated. Since the child-study team came up with an IEP that covered Jason's needs, I decided to let it go.

Then Jason hit seventh grade. With a multi-teacher schedule and changing classes, Jason's ADHD began to cause serious difficulties for him. Though the movement from class to class helped his inability to sit still, his poor organizational skills and short-term memory deficits became real problems. Once he left a class, he completely forgot any assignments he hadn't finished. Homework that did manage to make it home disappeared down a black hole and was never seen again.

The school sent out weekly down slips to the parents of students who were failing. Ours arrived every week like clockwork. It did little good, because there was never a list of missing work, and Jason couldn't remember what he hadn't turned in. I tried to set up a daily planner where Jason would write his assignments and the individual teachers signed off. It didn't work. I couldn't get him to write down his assignments and the teachers wouldn't back us, saying they didn't have time to check his planner let alone sign it. I tried numerous times to get some kind of a home/school connection put into the IEP, but the case manager always refused.

Reading was about the only class he was handling with any degree of success. Up until that time, Jason had been in Title I rather than special ed for reading. The program had worked well for him and he was able to read at about a sixth grade level. Unfortunately, Title I programs are only funded through sixth grade, so at the annual review Jason had to be moved into the resource room for reading.

At first I was ok with the move. Though it seemed a shame to pull him out of the only class where he was passing, I understood the school's position. I tried once again to get some sort of daily communication between home and school. The case manager refused to put it in the IEP, saying it couldn't be written as an objective. She did, however put a mention of it in the minutes and teachers promised to try. The

IEP had reasonable goals and objectives so once again we signed it.

That's when things began to go down hill. Suddenly Jason's reading scores took a nose dive right into the basement. In the Title I class Jason had managed B's, but now his grades were mostly F's with an occasional D. When I contacted the resource teacher, I discovered that rather than doing any kind of a placement test, she had put Jason in the same reading as the other students in her class. Normally that wouldn't have caused a problem. Unfortunately, the program she used was written at a fourth-grade level and tailor-made to send an ADHD kid straight up the wall. It required huge amounts of written work every day and employed a technique known as direct instruction.

With direct instruction, students read most of the text out loud. When they miscall a word, the teacher stops them and says, "That word is..." The student repeats the word and then rereads the entire section again. Jason had excellent comprehension skills, but he was not a good oral reader. In a typical reading session, Jason had to reread five or six times in a single paragraph. Then he was expected to do two to three pages of written work, which he rarely had time to finish in class and never remembered to bring home. Hence the F's. Not surprisingly, he became frustrated very quickly.

I should point out that the program the teacher was using is a very good reading program as is direct instruction; in fact, I've used both with great success. It just wasn't appropriate for Jason. Even worse, the reading materials were a full two years below what Jason had been reading in Title I. We decided he'd be better off in the regular classroom for reading. Though it would be a struggle for him, it more closely matched his learning style and he was sure to do better than he was.

When I tried to point these things out to the school personnel, they were less than sympathetic. For one thing, they refused to believe that he could read at a higher level even though he had been doing so in the Title I class. After all, he was failing at a fourth grade level; there was no way he could function at a higher one. Secondly, that particular reading program worked for *every* child; Jason was just being lazy. Since I don't believe *any* program works for *every* child and had seen Jason successful at a higher level, I wasn't willing to accept this.

To make a long story short, Jason got farther and farther behind and his situation became more desperate. Finally, the case manager agreed to meet with us. Since I was tired of the school's intimidation tactics, and it wasn't an official meeting, I asked that it only be the case manager, resource teacher, principal, and us. The case manager agreed, but when we arrived, the room was full of teachers. The only two missing were the two who had backed us in the past.

It was the meeting from Hell. Everything we suggested was rejected. They wouldn't even listen to the possibility that the reading program was wrong for Jason. It didn't matter anyway since the resource teacher said she simply couldn't run two reading groups at the same time. Nor could she give Jason a supervised study hall during the day when she had other students. I brought up Jason's ADHD repeatedly and was shot down every time. I clearly didn't understand what ADHD was since Jason showed *none* of the symptoms. It was obvious we had misunderstood the psychologist when he said Jason was the most classic ADHD child he had ever seen. Jason was emotional disturbed, always had been and always would be. It was time my husband and I accepted it and realized none of the things we were suggesting would do him the slightest good.

Tempers frayed, accusations began flying, and the meeting disintegrated into a shouting match. I would like to tell you that I calmly rose to my feet, declared the meeting at an end, and swept majestically out of the room. Unfortunately, it wouldn't even be close to the truth. I can't recall my actual words, but I do remember informing them in a rather loud voice that I was exercising my right as a parent to call for a re-evaluation and that I'd be contacting the state department of education to set up a due process hearing. I think I may have even slammed the door behind me as I stomped out.

Once I was out in the hall, reality hit. I'll never forget the horrible, sick feeling in the pit of my stomach as I looked up at my husband and said, "How in heaven's name are we going to send Jason back here tomorrow?"

According to the law, once the hearing process is started, the current IEP remains in effect. Not only did they continue to use the same reading program, they belatedly decided to use our idea for daily communication. Unfortunately they used it as a punish-ment instead of an organization tool. If Jason forgot to get his book signed by even one teacher he wound up in lunch detention. There were a few teachers who truly tried to help Jason by reminding him to get his assignment book signed but not all. A couple even refused to sign when he asked, saying they didn't have time right then. Jason always forgot to ask a second time and he spent every day in lunch detention. He was so isolated from the other students that when his best friend's father was killed in an accident, Jason didn't know about it until a week after the funeral.

Meanwhile a re-evaluation was done. Horrified by how the case manager had misinterpreted his previous report, the psychologist left no room for doubt in his diagnosis of ADHD. The academic tests backed us up, too. Though Jason's oral reading was low, his reading comprehension was almost a year above grade level. Since Jason no longer qualified as Emotionally Disturbed and he didn't have enough of a discrepancy to be called L.D., the school was faced with a dilemma. The only way he qualified for Special ed services was if they chose to recognize the ADHD diagnosis.

At a pre-hearing meeting set up by the hearing officer, I faced the school's case manager across the table for the first time since the re-evaluation had been finished. Her presentation included a great deal of impressive rhetoric and some classy side-stepping but never actually touched on the labeling issue.

Deciding it was time to pin her down, I folded my arms and looked her straight in the eye. "It seems to me that you have two choices," I said. "Either he's ADHD or he's not. If he's ADHD, you'll have to provide a study hall and an appropriate reading program for him. If he's not, he won't qualify for anything, and he's back in the regular classroom. So which is it?"

She was silent for several minutes then gritted her teeth and said, "He's ADHD."

My feeling of victory lasted all of ten seconds until the hearing officer said, "Could someone please explain to me what ADHD is?"

It's hard to say what would have happened had we gone through with the hearing, since the whole case hinged on whether Jason was ADHD or not. In the end we didn't actually go to a hearing. We were able to transfer him to the neighboring school district where I worked.

The way our state law is written, the new district may use the evaluation information to create a new IEP. Interestingly enough, when it came time for that first meeting, the new school proposed almost exactly the program we had asked for before we'd even had any chance for input. Needless to say we signed without hesitation. As for the new program, it worked like a charm.

When parents and schools districts fight, the children are ultimately the losers. Though I can't predict what the outcome of the hearing would have been, I do know it would have been nearly impossible for Jason to get a fair shake in that school district. By the same token, we gained nothing by keeping silent. We kept our mouths shut for three years and things just kept getting progressively worse for Jason.

Still, no matter what the outcome of the hearing, the district would have had to change Jason's IEP to reflect the new ADHD label and set up a program that addressed those needs. Even if it wasn't exactly what we wanted, it would have been an improvement.

Hopefully you will never find yourself in the position of calling for a hearing. Even so, it is a good idea to know what your rights, or procedural safeguards, are. School districts provide parents with a copy at each meeting. You will also find a complete copy taken directly from the IDEA law in Appendix 2. Appendix 3 contains the portion of the law outlining due process hearing.

I wish I could give you a step-by-step procedure to follow when disagreements arise. Unfortunately, rules and regulations vary greatly from state to state. A copy of those rules and regulations should be available from your school district or your state department of education. There are, however, things you can keep track of to ensure your child's needs are being met and precautions you can take to cover your bases should the need for a hearing arrive.

1. Know your rights and advocate for your child. Children with severe handicaps tend to have their needs met better than children with learning disabilities simply because their parents know the law and make sure school districts comply.

2. Your child should have a new IEP every year. The meeting must be held before the day and month on the previous year's IEP unless you sign permission for an extension. This is not just a rubber stamp for the pervious IEP. A new IEP should be developed and the goals and objects should reflect the goals and objects that are being taught in the regular classroom.

3. Progress on each objective should be documented and reported to you as often as grades come out (report card time).

4. Every three years your child must be reevaluated and relabeled. Insist on both IQ and academic testing, as well as testing for any other special service your child receives or that you think they may need.

5. Keep every official piece of paper you receive from the school including invitations to child-study meetings. I have an entire file cabinet drawer dedicated to school documents.

6. Document, document, document. Write down or record every conversation and phone call. Also write down what the weather is outside. Since weather information can be verified

by the weather bureau, your documentation will stand up in a court of law. Make copies of all correspondence, and put everything in writing so it will never come down to "their word against yours".

7. At the first sign of trouble, get in touch with your local P&A and/or PIC (See the next section.)

Help for Beleaguered Parents

The good news is, you don't have to go it alone. Every state in the nation has organizations that parents can go to for help. Two of the best are P&A's (protection and advocacy agencies for person's with disabilities) and PICs (Parent Information Centers).

The Protection & Advocacy System (P&A) was created by Congress in 1977 to implement the mandates of federal laws like as IDEA. Their services include:

1) investigating complaints;

2) informing people with disabilities about their civil rights and ways to enforce those rights;

3) representing people in meetings, negotiation sessions, administrative and judicial proceedings;

4) referring people to other sources of help

At the time of our difficulties with Jason, our local P&A's purpose was to provide protection and advocacy services for individuals with Developmental Disabilities. Now, however, their services usually extend to students with Learning Disabilities as well. You will have to check with your local P&A to see what services are available in your area.

P&A advocates know the law inside out and backwards. Best of all, they will attend child-study meetings with you and advocate for your child. As an educator, I have to admit the P&A people tend to make schools rather nervous because they are so very good at what they do. As a parent, I recommend you contact your local P&A at the first sign of trouble.

The purpose of a Parent Training Center (or Parent Information Center- PIC) is just what it sounds like. They assist parents/guardians of K-12 students in obtaining training and information about available programs, services, and resources statewide. They are run by parents, for parents, and are a great source for books, classes, videos, support groups, etc. Many publish a newsletter with pertinent articles about what is going on in your state concerning disabilities.

Like P&A, PICs often have people available who will accompany you to child-study meetings. Though not as well trained as P&A representatives, they are knowledgeable individuals who have children with special needs of their own, and are old hands at attending child-study meetings.

A list of P&A's and PIC's by state is available in APPENDIX I. Some pertinent internet sites are listed in Chapter 15.

504's
Even if everyone on the child-study team agrees, problems can arise. The laws governing special education go to great lengths to prevent schools from using special education as a dumping ground for kids with problems. The rules and regulations were written to keep kids out of special ed and they do an excellent job of it. If the child doesn't meet specific criteria, which varies from state to state, from district, and even from school to school, he or she can not receive special education services. No matter how well intentioned the school personnel, they are bound by the law, and can not place a child in special education even though they heartily agree he needs help.

There is, however, a loophole in the law. This loophole is Section 504 of the Rehabilitation Act of 1973. Basically, the law prohibits discrimination on the basis of disabilities in any program receiving federal funds.

In a nutshell, it says that schools which receive federal funds must provide services for students who don't qualify for special education as long as he/she meets the criteria. The law defines eligibility as any one who:

(1) has a physical or mental impairment that substantially limits one or more major life activities. Major life activities

include walking, seeing, hearing, *speaking*, breathing, *learning*, working, caring for oneself, and performing manual tasks.

(2) has a record of such an impairment, (such as a former label of L.D. This is particularly handy if a three-year re-evaluation doesn't show enough of a discrepancy to call the student L.D.)

(3) is regarded as having such an impairment.

One important distinction is that a student doesn't have to qualify for special education to qualify for a 504. Though it seems fairly straight forward, many school districts are reluctant to provide services through 504's because there is no funding for it. If your child is labeled as handicapped and receives speech therapy, special ed, occupational therapy, physical therapy, or counseling, the schools are reimbursed for a large portion of expense. If the same services are provided through a 504, the school district has to absorb the cost with no help from the Federal Government. Some of those services are inexpensive but many are quite costly.

Another problem parents run into with 504's is that many administrators don't have a good understanding of the law. There are a variety of ways to interpret *'an impairment that substantially limits one or more major life activities.'* As a teacher, I've gone rounds with one administrator who insists 504's only pertain to children with medical problems and another who doesn't see reading, writing, or math as life skills.

The good news is, 504's are there for students who don't qualify for special ed, though you may have to push to get it for them. Even the most reluctant school districts would rather write a 504 than face a lawsuit, especially one they are likely to lose.

So how do you, as a parent, force a school district to test, reevaluate, change an IEP, or provide 504 services?

First, do your homework. Contact your local PIC Make sure that what you are asking for is within the school district's power to provide. Most schools truly do have your child's best interests at heart, though they may not have the same perception of what those needs are as you do.

Second, be willing to compromise. Sometimes even the most difficult disagreement can be worked out if both sides are willing to give a little. The situation with my son Paul, for instance, was solved in a way neither side anticipated at the beginning. It wasn't perfect, but it worked.

Third, don't be afraid to stand up for what you believe. My only regret in the fiasco over Jason is that I didn't blow the whistle three years earlier when we first starting having difficulties. By keeping my mouth shut, I only prolonged the agony. In the end, the final blow-up was ten times worse than it would have been had I challenged the school district sooner.

Fourth, contact your local PIC and P&A. Both are incredible resources for all kinds of information. More importantly, they provide support for parents. School personnel respect advocates. Everybody tends to be on their best behavior when an advocate is present. As a parent who still has battle scars from meetings that got out of hand, I can't begin to tell you how much the support of a knowledgeable person at a child-study meeting is worth.

And last but definitely not least, no matter what you do when problems arise, keep focused on what is important: your child and his or her education.

Please return to:
Parent Information Center
5 North Lobban
Buffalo, WY 82834
1-800-660-9742

Chapter 15

Resources

Where can I go for help? Addresses for Pertinent internet sites are listed below. Since websites come and go on the internet so rapidly, you may want to do a "search" for Learning Disabilities, Dyslexia, or other specific learning disabilities. There is a wealth of information out there.

http://www.lindamoodbell.com/definitions/index.html
This site contains definition of most terms used in the field of learning disabilities.

The ERIC Clearinghouse on Disabilities and Gifted Education (ERIC EC)
The Council for Exceptional Children
1920 Association Drive
Reston, VA 20191
Toll Free: 1.800.328.0272
TTY: 703.264.9449
E-mail: ericec@cec.sped.org
Internet: http://ericec.org

Learning Disabilities Explained
http://www.ldpride.net/ldexplained.htm

Learning Disabilities Association
http://www.ldanatl.org/

L. D. On Line
http://www.ldonline.org/index.html

This website contains the law from which Special Education comes.
IDEA stands for Individuals with Disabilities Education Act.
http://www.ed.gov/offices/OSERS/IDEA/the_law.html

Irlen Institute
5380 Village Rd.
Long Beach, CA 90808
(526) 496-2550
www.irlen.com

How to Teach Math Facts & Strategies to All Students materials available through:
Mastering Math Facts
Western Washington, University
Bookstore- Mailstop 90
Bellingham, WA 98225-90
Fax: (360) 650-2888
Phone: (360) 650- 7443

TouchMath® materials & catalog available through:
Innovative Learning Concepts, Inc.
6760 Corporate Drive
Colorado Spring, CO 80919-1999
Phone: 1-800-888-9191

Reading By the Colors by Helen Irlen
Government web site for the Special Ed Law IDEA (Individuals with Disabilities Education Act)
www. Ed.gov/offices/OSERS/IDEA/the_law.html

FEDERAL AGENCIES

Administration on Developmental Disabilities
(PADD Program)
Hubert H. Humphrey Building
200 Independence Avenue, S.W.
Washington, D.C. 20201
Phone: (202)690-6905

Center for Mental Health Services
(PAIMI Program)
Parklawn Building
5600 Fishers Lane, Rm. 15-C-26
Rockville, MD 20857
Phone: (301)443-3667

National Institute on Disability and Rehabilitation Research
(PAAT Program)
Switzer Building 330 C Street, S.W.
Washington, D.C. 20202
Phone: (202)205-5666

Rehabilitation Services Administration
(CAP/PAIR)
Switzer Building, Rm. 3231
330 C Street, S.W.
Washington, D.C. 20202-2735
Phone: (202)205-8719

WEB SITES
www.protectionandadvocacy.com.htm
connected to websites of P&A's around the country

Learning Disabilities Association
www.ldnatl.org
connected to state and local LDA websites

National Center For Learning Disabilities www.ld.org
L.D. Resources www.ldresources.com
Schwab Learning Organization www.schwablearning.org-
Council for Learning Disabilities www.cldinternational.org
Council for Exceptional Children www.cec.sped.org
L. D. Information and Education Center www.ldiec.net
www.special-minds.com
All Kinds of Minds www.allkindsofminds.org
International Dyslexia Foundation http://www.interdys.org/index.jsp
L.D. Pride. www.ldpride.net
Learning Disabilities Association of California. http://quicksitebuilder.cnet.com/ldaca/
Smart Kids with Learning Disabilities http://smartkidswithld.org/
NLDLine- http://nldline.com/

Glossary

504's- Section 504 of the Rehabilitation Act of 1973. It provides services for non-handicapped students. Also refers to individual educational plan for such a student.

ADD- Attention Deficit Disorder- A condition caused by a lack of a chemical neurotransmitter in the nervous system. Typified by difficulty staying on task and wandering attention.

ADHD- Attention Deficit Hyperactive Disorder- A condition caused by a lack of a chemical neurotransmitter in the nervous system. Typified by difficulty staying on task and hyperactivity.

annual review- a review of the current IEP. These meetings must be held within a year of the original IEP and includes documentation of goals and objectives, review of service and the creation of a new IEP.

BIT (Building Intervention Team)- A team of teachers used in some districts as the pre-referral stage. Their job is to suggest strategies and interventions for the regular teacher to try and to decide if a referral for testing is indicated..

CAP- Central auditory processing- the ability of the brain to understand and interpret information that is taken in through the ears

case manager- The person responsible for a specific IEP. They generally assign testing, set up meetings, collect documentation etc.

child study committee- *see IEP committee*

child study meeting – *see IEP meeting*

distractible- easily pulled off task

Due Process- A legal safety net set up for the child when parents and school don't agree on placement or services.

Due Process Hearing- A hearing before an impartial officer who makes a decision in a due process case. Though it may involve lawyers it is not performed in a court of law.

Dyscalculia. A severe difficulty in understanding and using symbols or functions needed for success in mathematics.

Dysgraphia-. A severe difficulty in producing handwriting that is legible and written at an age-appropriate speed.

Dyslexia-A severe difficulty in understanding or using one or more areas of language, including listening, speaking, reading, writing, and spelling.

Dysnomia- A marked difficulty in remembering names or recalling words needed for oral or written language.

Dyspraxia- A severe difficulty in performing drawing, writing, buttoning, and other tasks requiring fine motor skill, or in sequencing the necessary movements.

Early literacy- A reading program that teaches children to read by immersing them in the written word.

expressive language - Usually refers to language that is spoken

fine motor skills- Skills that require the use of small muscles- handwriting, typing drawing etc.

gross motor skills- Skills that require the use of large muscles- walking, running, jumping, swimming etc.

handicap- a disadvantage that makes achievement unusually difficult

handicapping condition- The label is given a child that qualifies for special education. There is a specific set of criteria that must be met for each handicapping condition.

hyperactive- considerably more active than normal- many hyperactive children have some part of their body moving at all times

hyperactivity- the tendency to move constantly

IDEA- . Public Law 105-17,- Individuals with Disabilities Education Act, the law governing the education of students with handicaps

IEP committee- A group of people, including the parent(s), teachers, and other professionals involved with the child. Together, they develop the IEP (Individual Educational Plan.)

IEP- Individual Educational Plan -A document created at the child study meeting that which outlines what kinds of services the student will receive, who will be providing those services and even what objectives the student will work on.

IEP meeting- A meeting at which an IEP is developed

Impulsivity- the tendency to act without thinking

inclusion- A special education placement where the student receives special education services inside the regular classroom

Independent evaluation- A new evaluation done by a different multidisciplinary team when results of the first are in dispute.

initial placement- The first time a child is placed in special services.

interim review- A child study meeting held between annual reviews in order to change services

IQ- Intelligence Quotient. The generally accepted measure of intelligence or problem solving ability. Average is considered to be between 95 and 105.

Irlen Syndrome- Scotopic Sensitivity Syndrome- a visual perceptual dysfunction affecting principally reading and writing based activities. This syndrome is impacted by glare, luminance, wavelength, print pattern and black/white contrast

long term memory- memory that contains information for more than a few hours. Memories of past events are stored in long term memory for instance.

MDT (Multiple Disciplinary Team)- A team of professional assigned to gather information, test, and lend their expertise in determining whether special services are called for. They may also assist in development of the IEP.

memory (see long term and short term memory)

neurons- tiny finger-like projections on nerve cells that transmit nerve impulses

neurotransmitter- a chemical responsible for transmitting nerve impulses between neurons

override- A document written by the multi-disciplinary team to place a child in services when he or she does not meet specific criteria for a handicap. It requires extensive documentation and must usually pass a committee before being approved.

parental rights- see procedural safe guards

phonetic reading program- A reading program that teaches reading through phonics

phonics- The representation of speech sounds by means of symbols.

procedural safe guards- Certain rights guaranteed to the parents by federal law (A copy can be found in Appendix 1)

Public Law 105-17- See IDEA

pullout program- A special education placement where the student receives special education services outside the regular classroom

receptive language -Usually refers to understanding language that is heard

re-evaluation- when a student is given a battery of tests by a multi-disciplinary team to determine whether the child is eligible for services. By law, re-evaluation must be given at least every three years

replacement program- a special education placement that takes the place of the regular classroom instruction.

Ritalin- a drug commonly used to treat attention deficit that acts as an artificial neurotransmitter

role playing- a strategy for teaching a variety of skills. Participants play different parts in a situation in order teach a certain idea. A teacher might play the part of a student, for example, to demonstrate the appropriate way to ask for directions.

service provider- A professional, such as a learning resource teacher, that provides a specific services under the IEP.

short term memory- Memories that are needed only for a short times, a list of items needed at the grocery store for example.

sight word- A word that is not phonetic and is recognized by sight (Examples-the, want, school)

social behavior- the way one acts when around other people

SSS- Scotopic Sensitivity Syndrome (see Irlen Syndrome)

STO- Short term objective. The small target skills service providers hope to accomplish during the course of the IEP.

Support class- a type of special education placement-a support program provides additional instruction or practice on whatever concept is being taught in the regular classroom

Synapse- the space between nerve cells

tactile input- Information that reaches the brain through the sense of touch.

APPENDIX 1
P&A and PIC Addresses

This list contains addresses of organizations specializing in support for parents of children with handicaps including learning disabilities. The list is arranged alphabetically by state and contains a listing of state P&A's (protection and advocacy agencies for person's with disabilities) as well as for state PICs (Parent Information Centers) nationwide.

NICHCY
National Information Center for Children and Youth with Disabilities
P.O. Bx 1492
Washington, DC. 20013
Phone: (800) 695-2085
(202)884-8200
e-mail: nichcy@aed.org
Web site: www.nichcy.org

ALABAMA
Protection & Advocacy
Division of Rehabilitation Services
2125 E. South Blvd
Montgomery, AL 36116
Phone: 1-800-228-3231 (in state)
1-800-441-7607 (out-of-state)
Fax: (334)288-1104
E-Mail:jnorsworthy@sacap.org
Website: http://www.sacap.org

PADD/PAIMI/PAIR/PABBSS/
TBI/PAVA
Alabama Disabilities Advocacy program.
University of Alabama

Box 870395
Tuscaloosa, Al 35487-0395
Phone: (205)348-4928
Tdd: (205)348-9484
1-800-826-1675 (in state only)
Fax: (205)348-3909
E-Mail: egillesp@law.ua.edu
Web: www.adap.net

Parent centers
Special Education Action Committee Inc.
600 Bel-Air Blvd, Suite 210
P.O. Bx 161274
Mobile, AL 36616-2274
Phone: 251-478-1208
1-800-222-7322 (In AL)
Fax: (215)-473-7877
E-Mail: seacofmobile@seacpac.com
Web: www.seacparentassistancecenter.com

Learning Disabilities Assoc.

LDA of Alabama
P.O. Bx 11588
Montgomery, AL 36111

ALASKA
Protection & Advocacy
CAP
ASIST, Inc.
2900 Boniface Parkway, #100
Anchorage, AK 99504-3195
Phone: 907-333-2211
800-478-0047
Fax: (907)333-1186
E-Mail: akcap@alaska.com

Disabilities Law Center of Alaska
3330 Artic Blvd., Suite 103
Anchorage, AK 99503
Phone: 907-565-1002
1-800-478-1234 (in AK only)
Fax: (907)565-1000

E-mail: dflleurant@dlcak.org
Website: www.dlcak.org

Parent centers
PARENTS, Inc.
4743 E. Northern Lights Blvd.
Anchorage, AK 99508
907-337-7678Voice
907-337-7629TDD
907-337-7671
FAX:1-800-478-7678 in AK
E-mail:parents@parentsinc.org
Website: www.parentsinc.org

LINKS-MatSu Parent Resource Center
PO Box 876007
Phone: (907-373-3632
Fax: (907)373-3620
E-mail: links@gci.net
Web: www.linksprc.org

AMERICAN SAMOA
Protection & Advocacy
Client Assistance Program and Protection & Advocacy
P.O. Bx 3937
Pago Pago, AS 96799
Phone: 011-684-633-2441
Fax: (011)684-633-7286
E-Mail: marie@samoatelco.com

Parent centers
American Samoa CPRC
P.O. Box 2191
Pago Pago, AS 96799
Phone: 684-699-6621
E-Mail: suisala@blueskynet.as cfidd@Samoatelco.com
Web: http://www.taalliance.org/ptis/amsamoa

ARIZONA
Protection & Advocacy
Arizona Center for Disability Law
100 North Stone Ave, Suite 305
Tucson, AZ 85701
Phone: (520)327-9547

1-800-922-1447
Fax: (520)884-0992
E-mail: lcohen@acdl.com
Web: www.acdl.com

Parent centers
RAISING Special Kids
2400 North Central Ave, Suite 200
Phoenix, AZ 85004
Phone: (602)242-4366
Fax: (602)242-4306
1-(800) 237-3007 (in AZ)
email: info@raisingspecialkids.org
website: www.raisingspecialkids.org

Pilot Parents of Southern Arizona
2600 North Wyatt Drive
Tucson, AZ 85712
Phone: (520) 324-3150
1-877-365-7220
Fax: (520)324-3152
E-Mail: ppsa@pilotparents.org
Web: www.pilotparents.org

Families reaching Harmony, Inc.
Thedia Michelle Gamble
P.O. Bx 5423
Window Rock, AZ 86515
Phone: (520) 729-2468
TMGengima@aol.com

ARKANSAS
Protection & Advocacy
Disability Rights Center.
1100 North University
Little Rock, AR 72207
Phone: (501)296-1775
1-800-482-1174 (nationwide)
Fax: (501)296-1779
E-mail: panda@akddisabilityrights.org
nanelleast@arkdisabilityrights.org
Web: www.akrdisabilityrights.org

Parent centers

Arkansas Disabilities Coalition
1123 S University Ave., Suite 225
Little Rock, AR 72204-1605
Phone: (501) 614-7020
1-800-223-1330 (AR only)
Fax: (501)614-9082
E-mail: adcwstovall@earthlink.net
Web: www.adcpti.org

FOCUS, Inc
2809 Forest Home Rd.
Jonesboro, AR 72401
Phone: (870) 935-2750
Fax: (870)931-3755
E-mail: focus_inc2@hotmail.com
Web: www.ArkansasPTI.org

Learning Disabilities Assoc.
LDA of Arkansas
P.O. Bx 7316
Little Rock, AR 72217

CALIFORNIA
Protection & Advocacy
CAP Director
Client Assistance Program
2000 Evergreen St.
Sacramento, CA 95814
Phone: (916) 263-7372
1-800-952-5544
(916)263-7465 tty
1-866-712-1085
Fax: 916(236)7464
E-mail: smentkow@dor.ca.gov
Web: www.rehab.cahwnet.gov

Protection & Advocacy, Inc.
100 Howe Ave., Suite 185N
Sacramento, CA 95825
Phone: (916) 488-9955 Admin office
(916)488-9950 Legal office
1-800-776-5746 (Nationwide)

Fax: (916)488-2635 or 9962
E-mail: legalmail@pai-ca.org
catherine.blakemore@pai-ca.org
Web: www.pai-ca.org

Parent centers
DREDF
2212 Sixth St.
Berkeley, CA 94710
Phone: (510) 644-2555
1-800-466-4232
Fax: (510)-841-8645
E-Mail: dredf@dredf.org
Web: www.dredf.org

Exceptional Family Support,
 Education and Advocacy Center
6402 Skyway
Paradise, CA 95969
Phone: (530) 226- 5129
1-888-263-1331
Fax: (530)226-5141
E-Mail: sklowrance@aol.com
Web: www.sea-center.org

Exceptional Parents Unlimited
4440 N. First St.
Fresno, CA 93726
Phone: (559) 229-2000
Fax: (559)229-2956
E-mail: bcoulbourne@exceptionalparents.org
Web: www.exceptionalparents.org

Central California
Loving Your Disabled Child
4528 Crenshaw Blvd.
Los Angeles, CA 90043
Phone: (323) 299-2925
E-Mail: info@lydc.org
Web: www.lydc.org

Matrix
94 Galli Drive, Suite C
Navato, CA 94949

Phone:(415) 884-3535
1-800-578-2592
Fax: (415)-884-3555
E-Mail: norat@matrixparents.org
Web: www.matrixparents.org
(Northern California w/ Parents helping parents, Santa Clara)

Parents Helping Parents of San Francisco
Lois Jones
594 Monterey Blvd.
San Francisco, CA 94127-2416
Phone: (415)-841-8820
Nine counties in the San Francisco area

Parents helping parents of Santa Clara
Mary Ellen Peterson
3041 Olcott St.
Santa Clara, CA 95054-3222
Phone: (408) 727-5775-
(408-727-7655 TDY
Fax: (408)727-0182
E-Mail: info@php.com
Web: www.php.com

Support for Families of Children with disabilities
2601 Mission #606
San Francisco, CA 94110-3111
Phone: (415)282-7494
Fax: (415)282-1226
E-Mail: jduenas@supportforfamilies.org
Web: www.supportforfamilies.org

TASK
100 West Cerritos Ave.
Anaheim, CA 92805
Phone: (714) 533-8275
Fax: (714)533-2533
E-Mail: taskca@aol.com

TASK, San Diego
4550 Kearny Villa Rd # 102
San Diego, CA 92123

Phone: (858) 874-2386
Fax: (858)874-0123
E-Mail: taskca@yahoo.com
Web: www.taskca.org

Parents of Watts
10828 Lou Dillion Ave
Los Angeles, CA 90059
Phone: (323)566-7556
Fax: (323)569-3982
E-Mail: egertonf@hotmail.com

Vietnamese Parents of Disabled Children Assoc Inc.
7526 Syracuse Ave
Stanton, CA 90680
Phone: (310)370-6704
Fax: (310)542-0522
E-Mail: hgnguyen@vpdca.org
Web: www.VPDCA.org

Learning Disabilities Assoc.
LDA of California
PMB #355
655 Lewelling Bl
San Leandro, CA 94579

COLORADO
Protection & Advocacy
The Legal Center
455 Sherman ST, Suite 130
Denver, CO 80203
Phone: (303) 722-0300
1-800-288-1376
Fax: (303)722-0720
E-mail: tlcmail@thelegal center.org
Web: www.thelegalscenter.org

Parent centers
PEAK Parent Center Inc.
611 North Weber, Suite 200
Colorado Springs, CO 80903
Phone: (719)531-9400
TDY: (719)531-9403

1-800-284-0251
Fax: (719)531-9452
E-Mail: info@peakparent.org
Web: www.peakparent.org

El Grupo Viada's Parent Resource Center
126 West 5th Ave.
Denver, CO 80204
Phone: (303)864-1900
800-284-0251
Fax: (303)864-0035
E-Mail: elgrupovida@peakparent.org
Web: www.peakparent.org

CONNECTICUT
Protection & Advocacy
Connecticut Office of P&A for Persons with Disabilities
60B Weston St
Hartford, CT 06120-1551
860-297-4300 Voice & TDD
1-800-842-7303 (in state only)
tdd:860-566-2102
Fax: (860)566-8714
E-mail: james.mcgaughey@po.state.ct.us
Web: www.state.ct.us/opapd/

Learning Disabilities Assoc.
LDA of Connecticut
99 Asylum Ave
Hartford, CT 06105

CPAC
338 Main St.
Niantic, CT.06357
Phone: (739)308-9860
1-800-445-2722 (in CT)
Fax: (860)739-7460
E-mail: cpac@cpacinc.org
Web: www.cpacinc.orge

DELAWARE
Protection & Advocacy
Client Assistance Program

United Cerebral Palsy, Inc.
254 East Camden-Wyoming Ave.
Camden, DE 19934
Phone: (302) 698-9336
1-800-640-9336
Fax: (302)698-9338
E-mail: capucp@magpage.com

Community Legal Aid Society Inc.
100 W. 10th St.
Wilmington, DE 19801
Phone: (302) 575-0660
Fax: (302)575-0840
E-mail: bhartman@declsi.org

Parent centers
Parent Information Center (PIC/DE)
5570 Kirkwood Highway
Willmington, DE 19808-5002
Phone: (302)999-7394
Fax: (302)999-7637
E-Mail: maghaz@picofdel.org
Web: www.picofdel.org

DISTRICT OF COLUMBIA
Protection & Advocacy
University Legal Services
220 I Street, NE, Suite 130
Washington, DC 20002
Phone: (202) 547-0198
Fax: (202)547-2083
E-mail: jbrown@uls-dc.com
Web: www.dcpanda.org

Parent centers
Advocates for Justice and Education
2041 Martin Luther King Ave. SE, Suite 205
Washington, D.C. 20020
Phone: (202) 678-8060
1-888-327-8060
Fax: (202)678-8062
E-mail: kim.jones@aje-DC.org
Web: www.aje-dc.ORG

DC Parent Training & Information Center
Holly Easterday Adams
817 Varnum St., NE
Washington, DC 20017
Phone: (202) 832-6860

FLORIDA
Protection & Advocacy
Advocacy Ctr. For Persons w/disabilties
The times Building Ste. 513
1000 N. Ashley Dr.
Tampa, FL 33602
Phone: (8i3) 233-2920
tdd 1-866-875-1837
1-866-875-1837
Fax: (813)233-2917
E-mail: info@advocacycenter.org
h.grisson@advocacycenter.org
Web: www.advocacycenter.org

Parent centers
Family Network on Disabilities
2735 Whitney Rd
Clearwater, FL 33760-1610
(727) 523-1130
1-800-825-5736 (FL only)
Fax: (-727)523-8687
E-Mail: fnd@fndfl.org
Web: www.fndfl.org

Parent to Parent of Miami, Inc.
7990 SW 117th Ave, Suite 201
Miami, FL 33183
Phone: (305) 271-9797
800-527-9552
Fax: (305)271-6628
E-mail: info@ptopmiami.org
Web: www.ptopmiami.org
Family Network on Disabilities of Fla Inc
2735 Whiteny Rd
Clearwater, FL 33760-1610
Phone: (727)523-1130
1-800-825-5736 (FL only)

Fax: (727)532-8687
E-mail: fnd@fndfl.org
Web: www.fndfl.org

GEORGIA
Protection & Advocacy
Georgia CAP
123 N. McDonough
Decatur, GA 30030
Phone: (404) 373-3116
Fax: (404)373-4110
E-mail: GaCAPDirector@theOmbudsman.com
Web: www.theOmbudsman.com

Georgia Advocacy Office, Inc
100 Cresent Center Parkway, Suite 520
Tucker, GA 30084
Phone: (404) 885-1234
1-800-537-2329 (nationwide)
Fax: (770)414-2948
E-mail: info@thegao.org
Web: www.thegao.org

Parent centers
Parents Educating Parents and Professionals for All Children PEPPAC)
8957 Highway 5. Suite B
Douglasville, GA 30134
Phone: (770) 577-7771
Fax: (770)577-77740
E-Mail: peppinc@peppinc.org
Web: www.peppinc.org

Learning Disabilities Assoc.
LDA of Georgia
P.O. Bx 1337
Rosewell, GA 30077

GUAM
Protection & Advocacy
Parent Agencies Network

J. Madarang Dental Bldg.
2238 Rout 16, Suite 1=B
P.O. Box 23474
GMF, Guam 96921
Phone: 1- 671-637-4227
Fax: 1-671-637-4211
E-mail: capguam@ite.net

Guam Legal Services
113 Bradley Place
Hagatna,, Guam 96910
Phone 1-671-477-9811
Fax: 1-671-477-1320
E-mail: glsc@netpci.com

HAWAII
Protection & Advocacy
Hawaii Disability Rights Center
900 Fort Street Mall, Suite 1040
Honolulu, HI 96813
Phone:(808) 949-2922
Fax: (808)949-2928
E-mail: info@hawauudusabilityrights.org
gary@hawaiidisabilityrights.org
Web: www.hawaiidisabilityrights.org

Parent centers
AWARE
200 N. Vineyard Blvd., Suite 310
Honolulu, HI 96817
Phone: (808) 536-9684
Fax: (808)537-6780
E-Mail: jschember-lang@ldahhawaii.org
Web: www.ldahawii.org

Learning Disabilities Assoc.
LDA of Hawaii
200 N. Vineyard Blvd., Suite 310
Honolulu, HI 96817

IDAHO
Protection & Advocacy
4477 Emerald, Suite B-100
Boise, ID 83706

Phone: (208) 336-5353
1-866-262-3462
Fax: (208)336-5296
E-mail: coadinc@cableone.net
jbaugh@cableone.net
Web: www.users.moscow.com/co-ad

Parent centers
Idaho Parents Unlimited, Inc.
600 North Curtis Rd. Suite 100
Boise, ID 83705
Phone: (208) 342-5884
1-800-242-4785
Fax: (208)342-1408
E-Mail: parents@ipulidaho.org
evelyn@ipulidaho.org
Web: www. ipulidaho.org

ILLINOIS
Protection & Advocacy
Illinois Client Assistance Program
100 N. First St., 1st floor
Springfield, IL 62702
Phone: (217) 782-5374
Fax: (217)524-1790
E-mail: DHSHRLOL@dsh.state.il

Equip for Equality Inc.
20 North Michigan Ave Suite 300
Chicago, IL 60602
Phone: (312) 341-0022
Tty: 1-800-610-2779
1-800-537-2632
Fax: (312)341-0295
E-mail: contactus@equipforequality.org
Web: www.equipforequality.org

Parent centers
Designs for Change
29 E Madison., Suite 950
Chicago, IL 60602
Phone: (312) 236-7252
1-800-851-8728
Fax : (312)236-7927

E-Mail: markse@designsforchange.org
Web: www.designsforchange.org

Family Resource Center on Disabilities
20 E. Jackson Blvd. Room 300
Chicago, IL 60604
Phone: (312) 939-3513
1-800-952-4199 (IL only)
Fax : (312)939-7297
E-Mail: frcdptiil@ameritech.net
Web: www.frcd.org

Family T.I.E.S. Network
Deb Kunz
830 South Spring
Springfield, IL 62704
Phone: (217) 544-5809
1-800-865-7842
ftiesn@aol.com
www.taalliance.org/ptis/fties

National Center for Latinos w/disabilities
Maria Elena Rodriguez-Sullivan
1921 South Blue Island Ave.
Chicago, IL 60608
Phone: (312) 666-3393
1-800-532-3393
ncld@ncld.com
homepage.interaccess.com/~ncld/

Learning Disabilities Assoc.
Chicago LDA
3400 W. 111th St. PMB 215
Chicago, IL 60655

INDIANA
Protection & Advocacy
Indiana Protection & Advocacy Services
4701 N. Keystone Ave., Suite 222
Indianapolis, IN 46204
Phone: (317)722-5555
1-800-622-4845
Fax: (317)722-5564

E-mail: tgallagher@ipas.state.in.us
Web: www.IN.gov/ipas

Parent centers
IN*SOURCE
809 N. Michigan St.
South Bend, IN 46601-1036
Phone:(574) 234-7101
1-800-332-4433 (in IN)
Fax : (574)2347279
E-Mail: insource@insource.org
Web: www.insource.org

IOWA
Protection & Advocacy
Client Assustance Program
Division on Persons w/Disabilities
Lucas State Office Building
Des Moines, IA 50310
Phone:(515) 281-3957
1-800-652-4298
Fax: (515)242-6119
E-mail: harlietta.helland@iowa.gov

Iowa P&A Service Inc.
950 Office Park Road, Suite 221
West Des Moines, IA 50265
Phone: (515) 278-2502
1-800-779-2502
Fax: (515)278-0539
E-mail: info@ipna.org
spiper@ipna.org
Web: www.ipna.org

Parent centers
Access For Special Kids (ASK)
321 E. 6th St.
Des Moines, IA 50309
Phone:(515)243-1713
1-800-450-8667
Fax : (515)243-1902
E-Mail: julie@askresource.org
Web: www.askresource.org

Family Link CPRC
Orpheum Building
520 Pierce St., Suite 360
Sioux City, IA 51101
Phone (712)255-7722
Fax: (712)239-4685
E-Mail: thompsonwyattfam@aol.com

KANSAS
Protection & Advocacy

Client Assistance Program
3640 S.W. Topeka Blvd., Suite 150
Topeka, KS. 66611
Phone: (785)266-8193
1-800-432-2326
Fax: (785)266-8574
E-mail: slzk@srskansas.org
Web: www.ink.org/public/srs/CAP

Kansas Advocacy & Protection Services
3745 SW Wannamaker Rd.
Topeka, KS. 66610
Phone: (785)273-9661
Fax: (785)273-9419
E-mail: rocky@ksadv.org

Parent Centers

Families Together, Inc.
3033 W. Second, Suite 106
Wichita, KS. 67203
Phone: (316) 945-7747
1-888-815-6364
Fax: (316)945-7795
E-Mail: connie@familiestogetherinc.org
Web: www.gfamiliestogetherinc.com

KENTUCKY
Protection & Advocacy

Client Assistance Program
209 St. Clair, 5th Floor
Frankfort, KY 40601
Phone: (502) 564-8035
1-800-633-6283
Fax: (502)564-2951

E-mail: VickiL.Staggs@ky.gov
Web: http//kycap.ky.gov

Office for Public Advocacy
Division for P&A
100 Fair Oaks Lane, 3rd Floor
Frankfort, KY 40601
Phone: (502) 564-2967
1-800-372-2988 tdd (nationwide
Fax: (502)564-0848
E-mail: MaureenFitzgerald@ky.gov
Web: www.kypa.net

Parent centers
KY Special Parent Involvement Network (KY-SPIN)
10301 B Deering Rd.
Louisville, KY 40272
Phone: (502) 937-6894
1-800-525-7746
Fax: (502)937-6464
E-Mail: spininc@kyspin.com
Web: www.kyspin.com

FIND of Louisville
1146 South Third St.
Louisville, KY 40203
Phone: (502)584-1239
Fax L 502)-584-1261
E-mail: find@councilonmr.org
Web: www.findoflouisville.org

LDA

2210 Goldsmith Lane #22
Louisville, KY 40218

Louisiana
Protection & Advocacy
Advocacy Center
225 Baronne St., Suite 2112
New Oreleans, LA 70112-2112
Phone: (504)522-2337
1-800-960-7705 (nationwide)
Fax: (504)522-5507
E-mail: lsimpson@advocacyla.org

Web: www.advocacyla.org

Parent centers
Pyramid Parent training Program
2552 St. Phillip St.
New Orleans, LA 70119
Phone: (504) 827-0610
Fax: (504)827-2999
E-Mail: PyramidCPRC@aol.com

Project POMPT
4323 Division St, Suite 110
Metairie, LA 70002-3179
Phone: (504)888-9111
1-800-766-7736
Fax: (504)888-0246
E-Mail: carcenaux@projectprompt.com
Web: www.projectprompt.com

MAINE
Protection & Advocacy
CARES, Inc.
4-7 Water St., Suite 2
Hallowell, ME 04347
Phone: (207)622-7055
1-800-773-7055
Fax: (207)621-1869
E-mail: capsite@aol.com
Web: www.caresinc.org

Maine Advocacy Services
24 Stone St.
P.O. Bx 2007
Augusta, ME 04338
Phone: (207)-626-2774
1-800-452-1948
Fax: (207)621-1419
E-mail: advocate@drcme.org
kamoody@drcme.org
Web: www.drcme.org

Parent centers
Maine Parent Federation
P.O. Bx.2067

Augusta, ME 04338-2067
Phone: (207)623-2144
1-800-870-7746
Fax: (207)623-2148
E-Mail: parentconnect@mpf.org
Web: www.mpf.org

MARYLAND
Protection & Advocacy
Client Assistance Program
Maryland State Department
Division of Rehabilitation Services
2301 Argonne Dr.
Baltimore, MD 21218-1696
Phone: (410)554-9359
1-800-638-6243
Fax: (410)554-9362
E-mail: cap@dors.state.md.us

Maryland Disability Law Center
Central Maryland Office
The Walbert Building, Suite 400
1800 N. Charles St.
Baltimore, MD 21201
Phone: (410)727-6352
1-800-233-7201 (in state only)
Fax: (410)727-6389
E-mail: garyw@mdlcbalto.org
Web: www.mdlcbalto.org

Parent centers
Parents Place of Maryland Inc.
7484 Candlewood Rd, Suite S
Hanover, MD 21076-1306
Phone: (410)859-5300
Fax: (410)859-5301
E-Mail: info@ppmd.org
Web: www.ppmd

Learning Disabilities Assoc.
LDA of Maryland
P.O. Bx 526

Bowie, MD 20718-2236

MASSACHUSETTS
Protection & Advocacy
MA Office on Disability
Client Assistance Program
One Asburton Place, Rm 1305
Boston, MA 02108
Phone: (617) 727-7440
Fax: (617)727-0965
E-mail: Barbara.Lybarger@modi.state.ma.us

Christine Griffin, Exec Director
Disability Law Center, Inc.
11 Beacon St. Suite 925
Boston, MA 02108
phone: (617)723-8455
1-800-872-9992
tty: (617)227-9464
1-800-381-0577
Fax: 617(723-9125)
E-mail: cgriffin@dlc-ma.org
Web: www.dlc-ma.org/

Bob Fleischner. PAIMI Director
Center for Public Representation
22 Green St.
Northampton, MA 01060
Phone:(413)586-6024
hn5348@handsnet.org

Parent centers
Federation for Children with Special Needs
1135 Tremont St, Suite 420
Boston, MA 02120-2140
Phone: (617)236-7210
1-800-331-0688 (in MA)
Fax: (617)572-2094
E-Mail: fcsninfo@fcsn.org
Web: www.fcsn.org

Learning Disabilities Assoc.
LDA of Massachusetts

1275 Main St.
Waltham, MA 02451

MICHIGAN
Protection & Advocacy
Michigan P&A Service
4095 Legacy Parkwy, Suite500
Lansing, MI 48911-4263
Phone: (517)487-1755
1-800-288-5923 (in state only)
Fax: (517)487-0827
E-mail: ccerano@mpas.org
Web: www.mpas.org

Parent centers
CAUSE
6412 Centurion Dr. Suite 130
Lansing, MI 48917
Phone: (517)-886-9167
1-800-221-9105 (in MI)
Fax: (517)886-9366
E-mail: info@causeonline.org
Web: www.causeonline.org

Parents are Experts
Jessi Mullins
23077 Greenfield Rd. Suite 205
SouthField, MI 48075-3745
Phone: (248) 557-5070
1-800-827-4843

LDA of Michigan
200 Museum Dr, Suite 101
Lansing, MI 48933-1914

Tri-County Partnership
NW Center
18100 Meyers, Suite 307
Detroit, MI 48235
Phone: 313-863-0813
1-800-298-4424
Fax: (313)863-8048
E-mail:I nfodetroit@causeonline.org

Association for Children's Mental Health
6900 McGraw
Detroit, MI 48210
Fax: (313)895-2867
E-mail: detroitacmh@somepa.org

MINNESOTA
Protection & Advocacy

Minnesota Disability Law Center
430 First Ave. North, Suite 300
Minneapolis, MN 55401-1780
Phone: (612) 332-1441
1-800-292-4150 (in state only)
Fax: (612)334-5755
E-mail: bjursik@midmnleagal.org
Web: www.mndlc.org

Parent centers
Pacer Center, Inc.
8161Normandale Blvd
Minneapolis, MN 55438-1044
Phone: (952) 838-9000
(952)838-0190 TTY
1-800-537-2237 (in MN)
Fax: (952)838-0199
E-mail: pacer@pacer.org
Web: www.pacer.org

MISSISSIPPI
Protection & Advocacy

Client Assistance Program
Easter Seal Society
3226 N. State St.
Jackson, MS 39216
Phone: (601)982-7051
Fax: (601)982-1951
E-mail: pposey8803@aol.com

Mississippi P&A System for DD
5330 Executive Place, Suite A
Jackson, MS 39206
Phone: (601)981-8207
1-800-772-4057
Fax: (601)981-8313

E-mail: info@mspas.com

Parent centers
Parent Partners
5 Old River Place
Jackson, MS 39202
Phone: ((601)354-3302
1-800-366-5707 in MS
Fax: (601)354-2426
E-mail: tburton@ParentPartners.org
Web: www.ParentPartners.org

Project Empower
136 South Popular Ave
P.O. Box 1733
Greenville, MS 38702-1733
Phone: (662)332-4852
1-800-337-4852
Fax: (662)332*1622
E-mail: empower@tecinfo.com

MISSOURI
Protection & Advocacy
Missouri P&S Services
925 S. Country Club Drive'UnitB-1
Jefferson City, MO 65109
Phone: (573)893-3333
1-800-392-8667
MO relay tdd: 800-735-2966
Fax: (573)893-4231
E-mail: mopasjc@earthlink.net
Web: www.moadvocacy.org

Parent centers
Missouri Parents Act(MPACT)
One West Amour,Suite 302
KansasCity, MO 64111
Phone: (816)531-7070
816-931-2992 TDD
Fax: (816)531-4777
E-mail: msavage@ptimpact.com
Web: www.ptimpact.com

LDA of Missouri

P.O. Bx 3303
Springfield, MO 65808

MONTANTA
Protection & Advocacy
Montana Advocacy Program
400 North Park, 2nd Floor
P.O. Box 1681
Helena, MT 59624
Phone: (406)-449-2344 Voice/TDD
1-800-245-4743
Fax: (406)449-2418
E-mail: bernie@mtadv.org
Web: www.mtadv.org

Parents Let's Unite for Kids
Katharin Kelker
516 N. 32nd Street
Billings, MT 59101
406-255-0540
406-255-0523 FAX
1-800-222-7585 in MT
plukinfo@pluk.org
www.pluk.org

Parent centers
Parents Let's Unite for Kids
516 N. 32nd Street
Billings, MT 59101
Phone: (406)255-0540
1-800-222-7585 in MT
Fax: (406)255-0523
E-mail: plukinfo@pluk.org
Web: www.pluk.org

NATIVE AMERICAN
Protection & Advocacy
PADD/PAIMI/PAIR/PABSS/TBI
Native American Protection & Advocacy Project
3535 East 30th St, Suite 201
Farmington, NM 87402
Phone: 505-566-5880
1-800-862-7271

Fax: (505)566-5889
E-mail: tyanan@dnalegalservices.org

Parent centers
Native American Families Together Parent Center
129 West Third
Moscow, ID 83843
Phone: (208)885-3500
1-877-205-7501
Fax: (208)885-3628
E-mail: NAFT@moscow.com
Web: www.nativefamilynetwork.com

Therese Yanan, Executive Director
DNA-People's Legal Services, Inc.
P.O. Box 392
Shiprock, NM 87410
Phone: 505-368-3216
Fax: 505-368-3220
E-mail: hn4857@handsnet.org

NEBRASKA
Protection & Advocacy
Client Assistance Program
PO Box 94987
Lincoln, NE 68509
Phone: (402)471-3656
1-800-742-7594
Fax: (402)-471-0117
E-mail: victoria@cap.state.ne.us

Nebraska Advocacy Services, Inc.
134 South 13th St., Suite 600
Lincoln, NE 68508
Phone: (402)-474-3183 Voice/TDD
1-800-422-6691
Fax: (402)-474-3274
E-mail: nas@nas-pa.org

Parent centers
PPTI Nebraska
3135 North 93rd S
Omaha, NE 68134-
Phone: (402)-346-0525

1-800-284-8520
Fax: (402) 934-1479
E-Mail: info@pti-nebraska.org
Web: www.pti-nebraska.org

NEVADA
Protection & Advocacy
Client Assistance Program
1820 E. Sahara Ave, Suite 109
Las Vegas, NV 89104
Phone: (702)486-6688
Fax: (702)486-6691
E-mail: mjmoroun@nvdetr.org

Nevada Advocacy & Law Center,
6039 Eldora Ave , SteC-3
Las Vegas, NV 89146
Phone: (702)257-8150
Tty:(702)-257-8160
1-888-349-3843 (nationwide)
Fax: (702)257-8170
E-mail: ndalc@earthlink.net (Las Vegas)
Jmayes9524@aol.com
reno@ndalc.org@aol.com
Web: www.ndalc.org

Parent centers
Nevada Parents Encouraging Parents (PEP)
2355 Red Rock St.
Las Vegas, NV 89146
Phone: (702)-388-8899
1-800-216-5188
Fax: ((702)388-2966
E-mail: pepinfo@nvpep.org
Web: www.nvpep.org

NEW HAMPSHIRE
Protection & Advocacy
CAP
Client Assistance Program
Governor's Commission for the
Handicapped
57 Regional Drive
Concord, NH 03301-9686

Phone: (603)271-2773
Fax: (603)271-2837
E-mail: bhagy@gov.state.nh.us
Web: www.state.nh.us/disability/caphomepage.html

Disabilities Rights Center
18 Low Avenue
Concord, NH 03302-4971
Phone: (603)228-0432
tdd: 1-800-834-1721
Fax: (603)225-2077
E-mail: advocacy@drcnh.org
Web: www.drcnh.org

Parent centers
Parent Information Center
P.O. Box 2405
Concord, NH 03302-2405
Phone: (603)224-7005 (Voice & TDD) 1-800-232-0986 in NH
FAX : (603)-224-4365
E-mail: hthalheimer@parentinformationcenter.org
Web: www.parentinformationcenter.org

NEW JERSEY
Protection & Advocacy
New Jersey P&A, Inc.
210 S. Broad Street, 3rd Floor
Trenton, NJ 08608
Phone: (609)292-9742
(in state only)
tty: 609-633-7106
Fax: (609)777-0187
E-mail: advocate@njpanda.org
smitchell@njpanda.org
Web: www.njpanda.org

Parent centers
Statewide Parent Advocacy Network (SPAN)
35 Halsey Street, 4th Floor
Newark, NJ 07102
Phone: (973)642-8100
1-800-654-SPAN
FAX: (973)-642-8080
E-mail:AutinD@aol.com

Df77starfish@aol.com
Web: www.spannj.org

NEW MEXICO
Protection & Advocacy
Protection & Advocacy, Inc
1720 Louisiana Blvd., NE Suite 204
Albuquerque, NM 87110
Phone: (505)256-3100 Voice/TDD
1-800-432-4682
Fax: (505)256-3184
E-mail: info@nmpanda.org
Web: www.nmpanda.org

> *Parent centers*
> Parents Reaching Out, Project ADOBE
> 1920 "B" Columbia Drive SE
> Albuquerque, NM 87106
> 505-247-0192 Voice & TDD
> 1-800-524-5176 in NM
> FAX: 505-247-1345
> E-mail: prodreamaker@aol.com
> Web: www.paretnsreachingout.org
>
> Abrazos Family Support Services
> P.O. Box 788
> Bernalillo, NM 87004
> Phone: (505)867-3396
> Fax: (505)867-3398
> E-mail: info@abrazosnm.org
> Web: www.abrazosnm.org

NEW YORK
Protection & Advocacy
NY Commission on Quality of
Care for the Mentally Disabled
for the Mentally Disabled
401 State St.
Schenectady, NY 12305
Phone: (518)-388-2892
1-800-624-4143 TDD

Fax: (518)388-2890
E-mail: marcelc@cqc.state.ny.us
garyo@cqc.state.ny.us
Web: www.cqc.state.ny.us

Parent centers
The Advocacy Center
590 South Ave.
Averill Court
Rochester, NY 14620
Phone: (585)546-1700
1-800-650-4967 (NY only)
Fax: (585)-546-7069 FAX
E-Mail: blackwell@advocacycenter.com
Web: www.advocacycenter.com
Statewide except for NY City.

NEW YORK
Advocates for Children of NY
151 West 3th Street, 5th Floor
New York, NY 10001
Phone: (212)947-9779
FAX: (212)-947-9790
E-mail: aespada@advocatesforchildren.org
Web: www.advocatesforchildren.org
Five boroughs of New York City

New York
Resources for Children with Special Needs
116 East 16th St, 5th Floor
New York, NY 10003
Phone: (212)677-4650
Fax: (212)-254-4070
E-mail: info@resourcesnyc.org
Web: www.resourcesnyc.org

New York
Sinergia/Metropolitan Parent Center
15 West 65th St., 6th Floor
New York, NY 10023
Phone: (212)496-1300
Fax: (212)-496-5608
E-Mail: dlash@sinergiany.org

Web: www.sinergiany.org
New York City & Long Island

New York (CPRC)
United We Stand
202 Union Ave, Suite L
Brooklyn, NY 11211
Phone: (718)302-4313
Fax: (718)302-4315
E-Mail: uwsofny@aol.com
Web: www.unitedwestandofny.org

LDA
Six local chapters; check website for one nearest you

NORTH CAROLINA
Protection & Advocacy
Client Assistance Program
North Carolina Department of Health & Human Resources
2807 Mail Service Center
Raleigh, NC 27699-2806
Phone: (919)-855-3600
1-800-215-7227
Fax: (919)715-2456
E-mail: Kathy.Brack@ncmail.net

Governor's Advocacy Council for
Persons with Disabilities
1314 Mail Service Center
Raleigh, NC 27699-1314
Phone: (919)733-9250 Voice/TDD
1-800-821-6922
Fax: (919)733-9173
E-mail: Allison.bowen@ncmail.net
Web: www.Gacpd.com

Parent centers
ECAC, Inc.
907 Barra Row, Suite 102 &103
Davidson, NC 28036
Phone: (704)892-1321
1-800-962-6817 NC only

Fax: ((704)892-5028
E-mail: mlacorte@ecacmail.org
Web: www.ecac-parentcenter.org/

F.I.R.S.T
P.O. Box 802
Asheville, NC 28802
Phone: (828)277-1315
877-633-3178
Fax: (828)277-1321
E-Mail: FIRSTwnc@aol.com

Hope Parent Resource Center/Burke County Parent Resource Center
300 Enola Rd.
Morganton, NC 28655
Phone: (828)438-6540 (Eng?Span)
(828)433-2825 (Hmog)
Fax: (828)433-2821
E-mail: vbdieter@charter.net

LDA

LDA of North Carolina
P.O. Bx 3542
Chapel Hill, NC 27515-3542

NORTH DAKOTA
Protection & Advocacy
Client Assistance Program
600 South 2nd Street, Suite 1 B
Bismarck, ND 58504-4038
Phone: (701)328-8947
1-800-207-6122
Fax: (701)328-8969
E-mail: CAP@state.nd.us
Web: www.state.nd.us/cap/

Advocacy Project
400 E. Broadway, Suite 409
Bismarck, ND 58501
Phone: (701)328-2970
1-800-472-2670
1-800-642-6694 (24 H.line-in state)

1-800-366-6888 TDD
Fax: (701)328-3934
E-mail: tlarsen@state.nd.us
Web: www.ndpanda.org

> ***Parent centers***
> Pathfinder Family Center
> Arrowhead Shopping Center
> 1600 2nd Ave. SW, Suite 19
> Minot, ND 58701-3459
> Phone: (701)-837-7500 voice
> (701)-837-7501 TDD
> FAX: (701)-837-7548
> 1-800-245-5840 ND only
> E-mail: ndpath01@ndak.net
> Web: www.pathfinder.minot.com

N. MARIANAS ISLANDS
Protection & Advocacy
Northern Marianas
Protection and Advocacy System, Inc.
P.O. Box 503529
Saipan, MP 96950-3529
Phone: 1-670-235-7274/3
Fax: 1-670-235-7275
E-mail: nmpasi@vzpacifica.net
Web: www.NMPASI.com

OHIO
Protection & Advocacy
Art Schlesinger, CAP Administrator
Client Assistance Program
Governor's Office of Advocacy for
People with Disabilities
35 East Chestnut Street, 5th Floor
Columbus, OH 43215-0400
Phone: (614)466-9956
1-800-228-5405
Fax: (614)752-4197

Ohio Legal Rights Service
8 East Long Street, 5th Floor
Columbus, OH 43215
Phone: (614)466-7264 Voice/TDD

1-800-282-9181
tty: 614-728-2553
1-800-858-3542
Fax: (614)644-1888
E-mail: Cknight@olrs.state.oh.us
Web: http://olrs.ohio.gov/ASP?HomePage.asproper

Parent centers
Child Advocacy Center
Cathy Heizman
1821 Summit Road, Suite 303
Cincinnati, OH 45237
(513)821-2400
(513) 821-2442 FAX
CADCenter@aol.com
Southwestern Ohio, Northern Kentucky, Dearborn County, Indiana

Ohio OCECD
Bank One Building
165 West Center St., Suite 302
Marion, OH 43302-3741
Phone: (740)382-5452 Voice & TDD
1-800-374-2806
Fax: (740)383-6421
E-mail: ocecd@gte.net
Web: www.ocecd.or g

OKLAHOMA
Protection & Advocacy
Client Assistance Program
Oklahoma Office of Handicapped
Concerns
2712 Villa Prom
Oklahoma City, OK 73107
Phone: (405)521-3756
1-800-522-8224
Fax: (405) 943-7550
E-mail: James.Sirmans@ohc.state.ok.us
Web: www.state.ok.us/~ohc?cap.htm

Oklahoma Disability Law Center, Inc.
2915 Classen Blvd., Suite 300
Oklahoma City, OK 73106

Phone: (405) 525-7755
1-800-880-7755
Fax: (405)525-7759
E-mail: odlcokc@flash.net
Web: www.oklahomadisabilitylaw.org

> ***Parent centers***
> Oklahoma Parent Center, Inc.
> 4600 Southeast 29th St. Suite 115
> Del City, OK 73115-4224
> Phone: (405)619-0500
> 1-877-53-IDEA (4332)
> Fax: (405)670-0776
> E-mail: okparentctr@aol.com
> Web: www.okparents.org

LDA
LDA of Oklahoma
P.O. Bx 2315
Stillwater, OK 74076

OREGON
Protection & Advocacy
Oregon Advocacy Center
620 SW Fifth Ave., 5th Floor
Portland, OR 97204-1428
Phone: (503)243-2081
1-800-452-1694
1-800-556-5351 TDD
Fax: (503)243-1738
E-mail: welcome@oradvocacy
bob@oradvocacy.org
Web: www.oradvocacy.org

> ***Parent centers***
> Oregon COPE Project
> Anne Brown
> 999 Locust St. NE
> Salem, OR 97303
> Phone: (503)581-8156 Voice & TDD
> (503)391-0429 FAX
> 1-888-505-COPE
> orcope@open.org

www.open.org/~orcope

Oregon PTI
2295 Liberty St, NE
Salem, Ore 97303-6755
Phone: (503)581-8156
1-888-505-2673 (OR only)
Fax: (503)391-0429
E-mail: orpti@open.org
Web: www.open.org/-orpti

PENNSYLVANIA
Protection & Advocacy
Center for Disability Law & Policy
1617 J.F.K. Blvd., Suite 800
Philadelphia, PA 19103
Phone: (215)-557-7112
1-888-745-2357
Fax: (215)-557-7602
E-mail: info@equalemployment.org

Pennsylvania P&A, Inc.
1414 N. Cameron Street, Suite C
Harrisburg, PA 17103
Phone: (717)-236-8110 Voice/TDD
1-800-692-7443
Fax: (717)-236-0192
E-mail: ppa@ppainc.org
Web: www.ppainc.org

Parent centers
Hispanos Unidos para Ninos Excepcionales
(Hispanics United for Exceptional Children)
166W. Lehigh Ave, Suite 400
Philadelphia, PA 19133-3838
Phone: (215)-425-6203
FAX (215)425-6204
E-Mail: hueinc@aol.com

Mentor Parent Program
P.O. Box 47
Pittsfield, PA 16340
Phone: (814)563-3470
1-888-447-1431 (in PA

Fax: (814)563-3445
E-Mail: gwalker@westpa.net
Web: www.mentorparent.org

PENNSYLVANIA
Parent Education Network
2107 Industrial Hwy
York, PA 17402-2223
Phone: (717)-600-0100 Voice & TTY
1-800-522-5827 in PA
FAX: (717)600-1801
E-mail: pen@parentednet.org
Web: www.parentednet.org

Pennsylvania
Parents Union for Public Schools
Janet Lonsdale
311 S. Juniper St., Suite 200
Philadelphia, PA 19107
Phone: (215)546-1166
(215)-731-1688 FAX
E-mail: ParentsU@aol.com

LDA
LDA of Pennsylvania
Toomey Building Bx 208
Uwchland, PA 19480

PUERTO RICO
Protection & Advocacy
Office of the Governor
Ombudsman for the Disabled
P. 0. Box 41309
San Juan, PR 00940-1309
Phone: (787)721-4299
787-725-2333
1-800-981-4125 9 (in state)
Fax: (787)-721-2455
E-mail: mmorales@oppi.gobierno.pr
jrocasiso@gobierno.pr
Web: www.oppi.gobierno.pr

Parent centers

APNI
P.O. Box 21280
San Juan, PR 00928-1280
Phone: (787)763-4665
1-800-981-8492
FAX (787)765-0345
E-Mail: centroinfo@apnipr.org
Web: www.apnipr.org

Rep Of Palau
Executive Director
Client Assistance Program
Bureau of Public Health
Ministry of Health
P.O. Box 6027
Koror, Republic of Palau 96940
Phone: 011-680-488-2813
Fax: 011-680-488-1211

RHODE ISLAND
Protection & Advocacy
Rhode Island Disability Law Center Inc
349 Eddy Street
Providence, RI 02903
Phone: (401)-831-3150
(401)-831-5335 TDD
1-800-733-5332 (in state)
tdd: 401-831-5335
Fax: (401)-274-5568
E-mail: rbabdusky@ridlc.org

Parent centers
RIPIN
175 Main Street
Pawtucket, RI 02860-4101
Phone: (401)727-4144 voice
1-800-464-3399 in RI
FAX (401)-727-0867
E-Mail: collins@ripin.org
Web: www.ripin.org

SOUTH CAROLINA
Protection & Advocacy
CAP

Office of the Governor
Division of Ombudsman & Citizen Services
1205 Pendleton St.
Columbia, SC 29211
Phone: (803)-734-0285
1-800-868-0040
Fax: (803)-734-0546
E-mail: mbutler@govepp.state.sc.us
lbarker@govepp.state.sc.us
Web: www.govoepp.state.sc.us/cap/

Protection & Advocacy for People
with Disabilities, Inc.
3710 Landmark Drive, Suite 208
Columbia, SC 29204
Phone: (803)-782-0639 Voice/TDD
1-866-275-7273
Fax: (803)-790-1946
E-mail: infor@protectionandadvocacy-sc.org
prevost@protectionandadvocacy-sc.org
Web: www.protectionandadvocacy-sc.org

Parent centers
Advocacy Coalition for Youth with Disabilities
Beverly McCarty
c/o Family Resource Center
135 Rutledge Ave.
PO Box 250567
Charleston, SC 29425
Phone: (843)-876-1519
(843)-876-1518 FAX
mccartyb@musc.edu
Tri-county: Charleston, Berkeley, and Dorchester

Parent Training & Resource Center
MUSC-College of Health Professions
19 Hagood Ave, Suite 910
P.O. Box 29425
Chareleston, SC 29425
Phone: (843)792-3025
Fax: (843)792-1107

E-mail: mccartyb@musc.ed
Web: www.ptrc.org

PRO-PARENTS
652 Bush River Road,, Suite 218
Columbia, SC 29210
Phone: (803)772-5688 Voice & TDD
1-800-759-4776 in SC
FAX (803)-772-5314
E-Mail: proparents@aol.com
Web: www.proparents.org

LDA

LDA of South Carolina
P.O. Bx 1592
Cayce, SC 29033

SOUTH DAKOTA
Protection & Advocacy
South Dakota Advocacy Services
221 South Central Avenue
Pierre, SD 57501
Phone: (605)-224-8294 Voice/TDD
1-800-658-4782 (in state)
Fax: (605)-224-5125
E-mail: kearn@sdadvocady.com
Web: www.sdadvocacy.com

Parent centers
South Dakota Parent Connection
3701 West 49th St., Suite 200B
Sioux Falls, SD 57106
Phone: (605)-361-3171 Voice & TDD
1-800-640-4553 in SD
FAX (605)-361-2928
E-Mail: lynnbf@sdparent.org
Web: **www.sdparent.org**

LDA

LDA of South Dakota

P.O. Bx 9760
Rapid City, SD 57709

TENNESSEE
Protection & Advocacy
Tennessee P&A, Inc.
P. 0. Box 121257
Nashville, TN 37212
Phone: (615)-298-1080 Voice/TDD
1-800-287-9636
Fax: 615-298-2046
Email: gethelp@tpainc.org
shirleys@tppainc.org
Web: www.tpainc.org

Parent centers
Nashville Family Alliance Center
111 North Wilson Blvd.
Nashville, TN 37205
Phone: (615)321-5699
Fax: (615)322-9184
E-Mail: hlu1030@aol.com
Web: www.SPAN-TN.org

Support and Training for Exceptional Parents, Inc. (STEP)
712 Professional Plaza
Greeneville, TN 37745
Phone: (423)-639-0125
 (432)636)-8217 TDD
1-800-280-STEP in TN
FAX (423)-636-8217
E-Mail: information@tnstep.org
Web: www.tnstep.org

TEXAS
Protection & Advocacy
Advocacy, Inc.
7800 Shoal Creek Blvd., Suite 171 -E
Austin, TX 78757
Phone: (512)-454-4816 Voice/TDD
1-800-252-9108
Fax: (512)-323-0902

E-mail: infoai@advocacyinc.org
mfaithfull@advocacyinc.org
Web: www.advocacyinc.org

Parent centers
El Valle CPRC
530 South Texas Blvd, Suite J
Weslaco, TX 78596
Phone: (956)-969-3611
1-800-680-0255 TX only
Fax: (956)-969-8761
E-mail: texasfiestaedu@tiagris.com
Web: www.tfepoder.org/el_valle.html

Special Kids, Inc (SKI)
P.O. Box 266958
Houston, TX 77207-6958
Phone: (713)-743-5355
Fax: (713)-643-6291
E-Mail: speckids@aol.com

TEXAS
Parents Supporting Parents Network
601 N Texas Blvd,
Weslaco, TX 78596
Phone: (956)-447-8408
1-888857-8688
Fax: (956)-973-9503
E-Mail: lpadilla@rgv.rr.com
Web: www.thearcoftexas.org

Partners Resource Network Inc.
1001 Main St. Suite 804
Lubbock , TX 79401
Phone: (806)-762-1434
1-877-762-1435 in TX
Fax: (806)-762-1628
E-Mail: wtxpen@sbglobal.net
Web: www.PartnersTX.org

Partners Resource Network Inc. (TEAM project)
2547 Blossom St.
San Antonio, TX 78217

Phone: (210) 832-8945
1-877-832-8945
Fax: (210)832 8959
E-Mail: partnersteam@sbcglobal.net
Web: www.PartnersTX.org

Project PODER
Yvette Hinojosa
1017 N. Main Ave., Suite 207
San Antonio, TX 78212
Phone: (210)-222-2637
(210)-475-9283 FAX
1-800-682-9747 TX only
poder@tfepoder.org
www.tfepoder.org
San Antonia, Hondo, & Catroville. Cameron, Hidalgo, Willacy, & Starr Counties.

LDA

LDA of Texas
1011 West 31st ST
Austin, TX 78705

UTAH

Protection & Advocacy
Disability Law Center
The Commonwealth Legal Center
205 North 400 West
Salt Lake City, UT 84103
Phone: (801)-363-1347 Voice/TDD
1-800-662-9080
Fax: 801-363-1437
E-mail: finelson@disabilitylawcenter.org
Web: www.disabilitylawcenter.org

Parent centers
Utah Parent Center
2290 East 4500 S., Suite 110
Salt Lake City, UT 84117-4428
Phone: (801)-272-1051
1-800-468-1160 in UT
(801)-272-8907
Fax: (801)272-8907
E-Mail: helen@utahparentcenter.org

Web: www.utahparentcenter.org

LDA
LDA of Utah
P.O. Bx 651052
Salt Lake City, Utah 84165-1052

VERMONT
Protection & Advocacy
CAP
Vermont Disability Law Project
57 North Main St., Suite 2
Rutland, VT 05701
Phone: (802)-775-0021
1-800-769-7459
Fax: (802)775-0022
E:mail: nbreiden@vtlegalaid.org

Vermont Protection & Advocacy
141 Main St., Suite 7
Montpellier, VT 05602
Phone: (802)229-1355
1-800-229-1355
1-800-834-7890 (nationwide)
Fax: (802)229-1359
E-mail: info@vtpa.org
epaquin@vtpa.org
Web: www.vtpa.org

Parent centers
Vermont Parent Information Center
1 Mill Street, Suite 310
Burlington, VT 05401
Phone: (802)658-5315
1-800-639-7170 in VT
Fax: (802)-658-5395
E-Mail: vpic@vtpic.com
Web: www.vtpic.com

VIRGIN ISLANDS
Protection & Advocacy
Executive Director

Virgin Islands Advocacy Agency
63 Estate Crane Carlton
Frederiksted, V1 00840
Phone: (340)772-1200
Tdd: (340)772-4641
Fax: (340)-772-0609
E-mail: info@ciadvocacy.org
alamont@justice.com
Web: www.viadvocacy.org

Parent centers

V.I. FIND
P.O. Box 11670
St. Thomas, US VI 00802
Phone: (340)-774-1662
Fax: (340)-775-3962
E-Mail: vifind@islands.vi
Web: www.taalliance.org/ptis/vifind/

VIRGINIA
Protection & Advocacy
Virginia Office for Protection & Advocacy.
1910 Byrd Ave, Suite 5
Richmond, VA 23230
Phone: (804)225-2042 Voice/TDD
1-800-552-3962 (Souther VA only)
Fax: (804)-662-7057
E-mail: millervc@vopa.state.va.us
Web: www.vopa.state.va.us

Parent centers
PADDA, Inc.
6320 Augusta Dr Suite 1200
Springfield, VA 22150
Phone: (703)923-0001
1-800-869-6782 VA only
Fax: (703)923-0030
E-Mail: takemoto@peatc.org
Web: www.peatc.org

PADDA, Inc
813 Forrest Dr., Suite 3

Newprot News, VA 23606
Phone: (757)591-9119
1-888-337-2332
Fax: (757)591-8990
E-Mail: mjacob@padda.org
Web: www.padda.org

LDA

LDA of Virginia
Randolph Towers #505
4100 N. 9th St.
Arlington, VA 22203

WASHINGTON
Protection & Advocacy
Client Assistance Program
2531 Rainer Ave. South
Seattle, WA 98144
Phone: (206)721-5999
1-800-544-2121
Fax: (206)721-4537
E-Mail: capseattle@att.net

Washington P&A System
315 Fifth Ave. S. Suite 850
Seattle, WA 98104
Phone: (206)324-1521 Voice/TDD
1-800-905-0209
Fax: (206)957-0729
E-mail: wpas@wpas-rights.org
Mstroh@wpas-rights.org
Web: www.wpas-rights.org

Parent centers
Parent to Parent Power
1118 S 142nd St.
Tacoma, WA 98444
Phone: (253)-531-2022
Fax: (253)-538-1126
E-Mail: yvone_link@yahoo.com
Web: www.p2ppower.org

Specialize Training of Military Parents
STOMP

6316 South 12th St., Suite B
Tacoma, WA 98465- 1900
Phone: (253)-565-2266 Voice & TTY
1-800-5PARENT
Fax: (253)-566-8052
E-Mail: stomp@washingtonpave.com
Web: www.stompproject.org
U.S. Military installations; and as a resource for parent centers and others needing information on this subject.

Washington PAVE
6316 South 12th St., Suite B
Tacoma, WA 98465- 1900
Phone: (253)-565-2266 Voice & TTY
1-800-572-7368
Fax: (253)-566-8052
E-mail: jbutts@washingtonpave.com
Web: www.washingtonpave.org

Rural Outreach
805 Southwest Alcora
Pullan,
WA 99163
Phone: (509)595-5440
E-Mail: routreach@adelphia.net

LDA

LDA of Washington
7919 159th Pl. NE
Redmond, WA 98052

WEST VIRGINIA
Protection & Advocacy
West Virginia Advocates, Inc.
Litton Bldg, 4th Floor
1207 Quarrier Street
Charleston, WV 25301
Phone: (304)-346-0847 Voice/TDD
1-800-950-5250
Fax: (304)346-0867
E-mail: wvainfo@wvadvocates.org
Bpeck@wvadvocates.org
Website: www.wavocated.org

Parent centers
West Virginia PTI
371 Broaddus Ave
Clarksburg, WV 26301
Phone: (304)-624-1436 Voice & TTY
1-800-281-1436 in WV
Fax: (304)-624-1438
E-mail: wvpti@aol.com
Web: www.wvpti.org

LDA

West Virginia LDA
542 Locust St.
New Martinsville, WV 26155

WISCONSIN
Protection & Advocacy
Client Assistance Program
2811 Agriculture Dr.
P.O. Box 8911
Madison, WI 53708-8911
Phone: (608)-224-5070
1-800-392-1290
Fax: (608)224.5069
E-Mail: Linda.vefoe@datcp.state.wi.us

Wisconsin Coalition for Advocacy
16 N. Carroll Street, Suite 400
Madison, WI 53703
Phone: (608)267-0214 Voice/TTD
tty: 1-800-928-8778
Fax: (608)267-0368
E-mail: (Madison) wcamsn@w-c-a.org
lynnb@w-c-aorg.
 (Milwaukee) wcamke@w-c-a.org
Website: www.w-c-a.org

Parent centers
Native American Family Empowerment Center
Don Rosin
Great Lakes Inter-Tribal Council, Inc.
2932 Highway 47N, P.O. Box 9

Lac du Flambeau, WI 54538
Phone: (715)588-3324
(715)588-7900
1-800-472-7207 (WI only)
drosin@newnorth.net

Parent Education Project of Wisconsin
S. Patrice Colletti, SDS
(cont.)
2192 South 60th Street
West Allis, WI 53219-1568
(414)-328-5520 Voice
(414)-328-5525 TDD
(414)-328-5530
1-800-231-8382 (WI only)
PMColletti@aol.com
members.aol.com/pepofwi/

Wisconsin Family Assistance Center for Education, Training and Support
Janis M. Serak
2714 North Dr. Martin Luther King Dr., Suite E
Milwaukee, WI 53212
Phone: (414)-374-4645
(414)-374-4635 TTD
(414)-374-4655 FAX
wifacets@execpc.com

Native American Family Empowerment Center
Great Lakes Inter-Tribal Council, Inc.
2932 Highway 47N, P.O. Box 9
Lac du Flambeau, WI 54538
Phone: (715)588-3324
1-800-472-7207 (WI only)
Fax: (715)588-7900
E-mail: drosin@glitc.org

Wisconsin
Parent Education Project of Wisconsin
S. Patrice Colletti, SDS
2192 South 60th Street
West Allis, WI 53219-1568
Phone: (414)328-5520 Voice
(414)328-5525 TDD

(414) 328-5530
1-800-231-8382 (WI only)
PMColletti@aol.com
members.aol.com/pepofwi/

Wisconsin FACETS (PTI)
Wisconsin Family Assistance Center for Education, Training, and Support
2714 North Dr. Martin Luther King Dr.
Milwaukee, WI 53212
Phone: (414)-374-4645
(414)374-4635 TTD
Fax: (414)374-4655
E-mail: wifacets@execpc.com
Web: www.wifacets.org

LDA
LDA of Wisconsin
1446 Baytree Lane
Neenah, WI 54956

WYOMING

Protection & Advocacy
320 West 25th Street, 2nd Floor
Cheyenne, WY 82001
Phone: (307) 632-3496
1-800-624-7648
Fax: (307) 632-3496
E-mail: wypanda@vcn.com
Web: http//wypanda.vcn.com

Parent centers
Parent Information Center
5 North Lobban
Buffalo, WY 82834
Phone: (307)684-2277 Voice & TDD
1-800-660-9742 WY only
Fax: (307)-684-5314
E-mail: tdawson@wpic.org
Web: www.wpic.org

www.wpic.org Parent Information Center

FEDERAL AGENCIES

Administration on Developmental Disabilities
(PADD Program)
Hubert H. Humphrey Building
200 Independence Avenue, S.W.
Washington, D.C. 20201
Phone: (202)690-6905

Center for Mental Health Services
(PAIMI Program)
Parklawn Building
5600 Fishers Lane, Rm. 15-C-26
Rockville, MD 20857
Phone: (301)443-3667

National Institute on Disability and Rehabilitation Research
(PAAT Program)
Switzer Building 330 C Street, S.W.
Washington, D.C. 20202
Phone: (202)205-5666

Rehabilitation Services Administration
(CAP/PAIR)
Switzer Building, Rm. 3231
330 C Street, S.W.
Washington, D.C. 20202-2735
Phone: (202)205-8719

WEB SITES

www.protectionandadvocacy.com/demofile.htm- connected to websites of P&A's around the country

Learning Disabilities Association
www.ldnatl.org
connected to state and local LDA websites

The ERIC Clearinghouse on Disabilities and Gifted Education (ERIC EC)
The Council for Exceptional Children

1920 Association Drive
Reston, VA 20191
Toll Free: 1.800.328.0272
TTY: 703.264.9449
E-mail: ericec@cec.sped.org
Internet: http://ericec.org

http://www.ed.gov/offices/OSERS/IDEA/the_law.html This website contains the law from which Special Education comes or IDEA (Individuals with Disabilities Education Act

Learning Disabilities Explained
http://www.ldpride.net/ldexplained.htm

Learning Disabilities Association
http://www.ldanatl.org/

L. D. On Line
http://www.ldonline.org/index.html

Irlen Institute
5380 Village Rd.
Long Beach, CA 90808
(526) 496-2550
Irlen.com (information on Scotopic Sensitivity or Irlen Syndorme)

How to Teach Math Facts & Strategies to All Students
materials available through::
Mastering Math Facts
Western Washington, University
Bookstore- Mailstop 90
Bellingham, WA 98225-90
Fax: (360) 650-2888
Phone: (360) 650- 7443

***TouchMath*®** materials & catalog available through:
Innovative Learning Concepts, Inc.
6760 Corporate Drive
Colorado Spring, CO 80919-1999
Phone: 1-800-888-9191

APPENDIX 2
Parent's Rights

SEC. 615. PROCEDURAL SAFEGUARDS

(a) ESTABLISHMENT OF PROCEDURES- Any State educational agency, State agency, or local educational agency that receives assistance under this part shall establish and maintain procedures in accordance with this section to ensure that children with disabilities and their parents are guaranteed procedural safeguards with respect to the provision of free appropriate public education by such agencies.

(b) TYPES OF PROCEDURES- The procedures required by this section shall include --

(1) an opportunity for the parents of a child with a disability to examine all records relating to such child and to participate in meetings with respect to the identification, evaluation, and educational placement of the child, and the provision of a free appropriate public education to such child, and to obtain an independent educational evaluation of the child;

(2) procedures to protect the rights of the child whenever the parents of the child are not known, the agency cannot, after reasonable efforts, locate the parents, or the child is a ward of the State, including the assignment of an individual (who shall not be an employee of the State educational agency, the local educational agency, or any other agency that is involved in the education or care of the child) to act as a surrogate for the parents;

(3) written prior notice to the parents of the child whenever such agency --

(A) proposes to initiate or change; or

(B) refuses to initiate or change; the identification, evaluation, or educational placement of the child, in accordance with subsection (c), or the provision of a free appropriate public education to the child;

(4) procedures designed to ensure that the notice required by paragraph (3) is in the native language of the parents, unless it clearly is not feasible to do so;

(5) an opportunity for mediation in accordance with subsection (e);

(6) an opportunity to present complaints with respect to any matter relating to the identification, evaluation, or educational placement of the child, or the provision of a free appropriate public education to such child;

(7) procedures that require the parent of a child with a disability, or the attorney representing the child, to provide notice (which shall remain confidential) --

(A) to the State educational agency or local educational agency, as the case may be, in the complaint filed under paragraph (6); and

(B) that shall include --

(i) the name of the child, the address of the residence of the child, and the name of the school the child is attending;

(ii) a description of the nature of the problem of the child relating to such proposed initiation or change, including facts relating to such problem; and

(iii) a proposed resolution of the problem to the extent known and available to the parents at the time; and

(8) procedures that require the State educational agency to develop a model form to assist parents in filing a complaint in accordance with paragraph (7).

(c) CONTENT OF PRIOR WRITTEN NOTICE- The notice required by subsection (b)(3) shall include --

(1) a description of the action proposed or refused by the agency;

(2) an explanation of why the agency proposes or refuses to take the action;

(3) a description of any other options that the agency considered and the reasons why those options were rejected;

(4) a description of each evaluation procedure, test, record, or report the agency used as a basis for the proposed or refused action;

(5) a description of any other factors that are relevant to the agency's proposal or refusal;

(6) a statement that the parents of a child with a disability have protection under the procedural safeguards of this part and, if this notice is not an initial referral for evaluation, the means by which a copy of a description of the procedural safeguards can be obtained; and

(7) sources for parents to contact to obtain assistance in understanding the provisions of this part.

(d) PROCEDURAL SAFEGUARDS NOTICE-

(1) IN GENERAL- A copy of the procedural safeguards available to the parents of a child with a disability shall be given to the parents, at a minimum --

(A) upon initial referral for evaluation;

(B) upon each notification of an individualized education program meeting and upon re-evaluation of the child; and

(C) upon registration of a complaint under subsection (b)(6).

(2) CONTENTS- The procedural safeguards notice shall include a full explanation of the procedural safeguards, written in the native language of the parents, unless it clearly is not feasible to do so, and written in an easily understandable manner, available under this section and under regulations promulgated by the Secretary relating to --

(A) independent educational evaluation;

(B) prior written notice;

(C) parental consent;

(D) access to educational records;

(E) opportunity to present complaints;

(F) the child's placement during pendency of due process proceedings;

(G) procedures for students who are subject to placement in an interim alternative educational setting;

(H) requirements for unilateral placement by parents of children in private schools at public expense;

(I) mediation;

(J) due process hearings, including requirements for disclosure of evaluation results and recommendations;

(K) State-level appeals (if applicable in that State);

(L) civil actions; and

(M) attorneys' fees.

(e) MEDIATION-

(1) IN GENERAL- Any State educational agency or local educational agency that receives assistance under this part shall ensure that procedures are established and implemented to allow parties to disputes involving any matter described in subsection (b)(6) to resolve such disputes through a mediation process which, at a minimum, shall be available whenever a hearing is requested under subsection (f) or (k).

(2) REQUIREMENTS- Such procedures shall meet the following requirements:

(A) The procedures shall ensure that the mediation process --

(i) is voluntary on the part of the parties;

(ii) is not used to deny or delay a parent's right to a due process hearing under subsection (f), or to deny any other rights afforded under this part; and

(iii) is conducted by a qualified and impartial mediator who is trained in effective mediation techniques.

(B) A local educational agency or a State agency may establish procedures to require parents who choose not to use the mediation process to meet, at a time and location convenient to the parents, with a disinterested party who is under contract with --

(i) a parent training and information center or community parent resource center in the State established under section 682 or 683; or

(ii) an appropriate alternative dispute resolution entity; to encourage the use, and explain the benefits, of the mediation process to the parents.

(C) The State shall maintain a list of individuals who are qualified mediators and knowledgeable in laws and regulations relating to the provision of special education and related services.

(2) the right to present evidence and confront, cross-examine, and compel the attendance of witnesses;

(3) the right to a written, or, at the option of the parents, electronic verbatim record of such hearing; and

(4) the right to written, or, at the option of the parents, electronic findings of fact and decisions (which findings and decisions shall be made available to the public consistent with the requirements of section 617(c) (relating to the confidentiality of data, information, and records) and shall also be transmitted to the advisory panel established pursuant to section 612(a)(21)).

(i) ADMINISTRATIVE PROCEDURES-

(1) IN GENERAL-

(A) DECISION MADE IN HEARING- A decision made in a hearing conducted pursuant to subsection (f) or (k) shall be final, except that any party involved in such hearing may appeal such decision under the provisions of subsection (g) and paragraph (2) of this subsection.

(B) DECISION MADE AT APPEAL- A decision made under subsection (g) shall be final, except that any party may bring an action under paragraph (2) of this subsection.

(2) RIGHT TO BRING CIVIL ACTION-

(A) IN GENERAL- Any party aggrieved by the findings and decision made under subsection (f) or (k) who does not have the right to an appeal under subsection (g), and any party aggrieved by the findings and decision under this subsection, shall have the right to bring a civil action with respect to the complaint presented pursuant to this section, which action may be brought in any State court of competent jurisdiction or in a district court of the United States without regard to the amount in controversy.

(B) ADDITIONAL REQUIREMENTS- In any action brought under this paragraph, the court —

(i) shall receive the records of the administrative proceedings;

(ii) shall hear additional evidence at the request of a party; and

(iii) basing its decision on the preponderance of the evidence, shall grant such relief as the court determines is appropriate.

(3) JURISDICTION OF DISTRICT COURTS; ATTORNEYS' FEES-

(A) IN GENERAL- The district courts of the United States shall have jurisdiction of actions brought under this section without regard to the amount in controversy.

(B) AWARD OF ATTORNEYS' FEES- In any action or proceeding brought under this section, the court, in its discretion, may award reasonable attorneys' fees as part of the costs to the parents of a child with a disability who is the prevailing party.

(C) DETERMINATION OF AMOUNT OF ATTORNEYS' FEES- Fees awarded under this paragraph shall be based on rates prevailing in the community in which the action or proceeding arose for the kind and quality of services furnished. No bonus or multiplier may be used in calculating the fees awarded under this subsection.

(D) PROHIBITION OF ATTORNEYS' FEES AND RELATED COSTS FOR CERTAIN SERVICES-

(i) Attorneys' fees may not be awarded and related costs may not be reimbursed in any action or proceeding under this section for services performed subsequent to the time of a written offer of settlement to a parent if --

(I) the offer is made within the time prescribed by Rule 68 of the Federal Rules of Civil Procedure or, in the case of an administrative proceeding, at any time more than 10 days before the proceeding begins;

(II) the offer is not accepted within 10 days; and

(III) the court or administrative hearing officer finds that the relief finally obtained by the parents is not more favorable to the parents than the offer of settlement.

(ii) Attorneys' fees may not be awarded relating to any meeting of the IEP Team unless such meeting is convened as a result of an administrative proceeding or judicial action, or, at the discretion of the State, for a mediation described in subsection (e) that is conducted prior to the filing of a complaint under subsection (b)(6) or (k) of this section.

(E) EXCEPTION TO PROHIBITION ON ATTORNEYS' FEES AND RELATED COSTS- Notwithstanding subparagraph (D), an award of attorneys' fees and related costs may be made to a parent who is the prevailing party and who was substantially justified in rejecting the settlement offer.

(F) REDUCTION IN AMOUNT OF ATTORNEYS' FEES- Except as provided in subparagraph (G), whenever the court finds that --

(i) the parent, during the course of the action or proceeding, unreasonably protracted the final resolution of the controversy;

(ii) the amount of the attorneys' fees otherwise authorized to be awarded unreasonably exceeds the hourly rate prevailing in the community for similar services by attorneys of reasonably comparable skill, reputation, and experience;

(iii) the time spent and legal services furnished were excessive considering the nature of the action or proceeding; or

(iv) the attorney representing the parent did not provide to the school district the appropriate information in the due process complaint in accordance with subsection (b)(7); the court shall reduce, accordingly, the amount of the attorneys' fees awarded under this section.

(G) EXCEPTION TO REDUCTION IN AMOUNT OF ATTORNEYS' FEES- The provisions of subparagraph (F) shall not apply in any action or proceeding if the court finds that the State or local educational agency unreasonably protracted the final resolution of the action or proceeding or there was a violation of this section.

(j) MAINTENANCE OF CURRENT EDUCATIONAL PLACEMENT- Except as provided in subsection (k)(7), during the pendency of any proceedings conducted pursuant to this section, unless the State or local educational agency and the parents otherwise agree, the child shall remain in the then-current educational placement of such child, or, if applying for initial admission to a public school, shall, with the consent of the parents, be placed in the public school program until all such proceedings have been completed.

(k) PLACEMENT IN ALTERNATIVE EDUCATIONAL SETTING-

(1) AUTHORITY OF SCHOOL PERSONNEL-

(A) School personnel under this section may order a change in the placement of a child with a disability --

(i) to an appropriate interim alternative educational setting, another setting, or suspension, for not more than 10 school days (to the extent such alternatives would be applied to children without disabilities); and

(ii) to an appropriate interim alternative educational setting for the same amount of time that a child without a disability would be subject to discipline, but for not more than 45 days if --

(I) the child carries a weapon to school or to a school function under the jurisdiction of a State or a local educational agency; or
(II) the child knowingly possesses or uses illegal drugs or sells or solicits the sale of a controlled substance while at school or a school function under the jurisdiction of a State or local educational agency.

(B) Either before or not later than 10 days after taking a disciplinary action described in subparagraph (A) --

(i) if the local educational agency did not conduct a functional behavioral assessment and implement a behavioral intervention plan for such child before the behavior that resulted in the suspension described in subparagraph (A), the agency shall convene an IEP meeting to develop an assessment plan to address that behavior; or

(ii) immediately, if possible, but in no case later than 10 school days after the date on which the decision to take that action is made, a review shall be conducted of the relationship between the child's disability and the behavior subject to the disciplinary action.

(B) INDIVIDUALS TO CARRY OUT REVIEW- A review described in subparagraph (A) shall be conducted by the IEP Team and other qualified personnel.

(C) CONDUCT OF REVIEW- In carrying out a review described in subparagraph (A), the IEP Team may determine that the behavior of the child was not a manifestation of such child's disability only if the IEP Team --

(i) first considers, in terms of the behavior subject to disciplinary action, all relevant information, including --

(I) evaluation and diagnostic results, including such results or other relevant information supplied by the parents of the child;

(II) observations of the child; and

(III) the child's IEP and placement; and

(ii) then determines that --

(I) in relationship to the behavior subject to disciplinary action, the child's IEP and placement were appropriate and the special education services, supplementary aids and services, and behavior intervention strategies were provided consistent with the child's IEP and placement;

(II) the child's disability did not impair the ability of the child to understand the impact and consequences of the behavior subject to disciplinary action; and

(III) the child's disability did not impair the ability of the child to control the behavior subject to disciplinary action.

(5) DETERMINATION THAT BEHAVIOR WAS NOT MANIFESTATION OF DISABILITY-

(A) IN GENERAL- If the result of the review described in paragraph (4) is a determination, consistent with paragraph (4)(C), that the behavior of the child with a disability was not a manifestation of the child's disability, the relevant disciplinary procedures applicable to children without disabilities may be applied to the child in the same manner in which they would be applied to children without disabilities, except as provided in section 612(a)(1).

(B) ADDITIONAL REQUIREMENT- If the public agency initiates disciplinary procedures applicable to all children, the agency shall ensure that the special education and disciplinary records of the child with a disability are transmitted for consideration by the person or persons making the final determination regarding the disciplinary action.

(6) PARENT APPEAL-

(A) IN GENERAL-

(i) If the child's parent disagrees with a determination that the child's behavior was not a manifestation of the child's disability or with any decision regarding placement, the parent may request a hearing.

(ii) The State or local educational agency shall arrange for an expedited hearing in any case described in this subsection when requested by a parent.

(B) REVIEW OF DECISION-

(i) In reviewing a decision with respect to the manifestation determination, the hearing officer shall determine whether the public agency has demonstrated that the child's behavior was not a manifestation of such child's disability consistent with the requirements of paragraph (4)(C).

(ii) In reviewing a decision under paragraph (1)(A)(ii) to place the child in an interim alternative educational setting, the hearing officer shall apply the standards set out in paragraph (2).

(7) PLACEMENT DURING APPEALS-

(A) IN GENERAL- When a parent requests a hearing regarding a disciplinary action described in paragraph (1)(A)(ii) or paragraph (2) to challenge the interim alternative educational setting or the manifestation determination, the child shall remain in the interim alternative educational setting pending the decision of the hearing officer or until the expiration of the time period provided for in paragraph (1)(A)(ii) or paragraph (2), whichever occurs first, unless the parent and the State or local educational agency agree otherwise.

(B) CURRENT PLACEMENT- If a child is placed in an interim alternative educational setting pursuant to paragraph (1)(A)(ii) or paragraph (2) and school personnel propose to change the child's placement after expiration of the interim alternative placement, during the pendency of any proceeding to challenge the proposed change in placement, the child shall remain in the current placement (the child's placement prior to the interim alternative educational setting), except as provided in subparagraph (C).

(C) EXPEDITED HEARING-

(i) If school personnel maintain that it is dangerous for the child to be in the current placement (placement prior to removal to the interim alternative education setting) during the pendency of the due process proceedings, the local educational agency may request an expedited hearing.

(ii) In determining whether the child may be placed in the alternative educational setting or in another appropriate placement ordered by the hearing officer, the hearing officer shall apply the standards set out in paragraph (2).

(A) Nothing in this part shall be construed to prohibit an agency from reporting a crime committed by a child with a disability to appropriate authorities or to prevent State law enforcement and judicial authorities from exercising their responsibilities with regard to the application of Federal and State law to crimes committed by a child with a disability.

(B) An agency reporting a crime committed by a child with a disability shall ensure that copies of the special education and disciplinary records of the child are transmitted for consideration by the appropriate authorities to whom it reports the crime.

(10) DEFINITIONS- For purposes of this subsection, the following definitions apply:

(A) CONTROLLED SUBSTANCE- The term 'controlled substance' means a drug or other substance identified under schedules I, II, III, IV, or V in section 202(c) of the Controlled Substances Act (21 U.S.C. 812(c)).

(B) ILLEGAL DRUG- The term 'illegal drug' --

(i) means a controlled substance; but

(ii) does not include such a substance that is legally possessed or used under the supervision of a licensed health-care professional or that is legally possessed or used under any other authority under that Act or under any other provision of Federal law.

(C) SUBSTANTIAL EVIDENCE- The term 'substantial evidence'means beyond a preponderance of the evidence.

(D) WEAPON- The term weapon' has the meaning given the term 'dangerous weapon' under paragraph (2) of the first subsection (g) of section 930 of title 18, United States Code.

(l) RULE OF CONSTRUCTION- Nothing in this title shall be construed to restrict or limit the rights, procedures, and remedies available under the Constitution, the Americans with Disabilities Act of 1990, title V of the Rehabilitation Act of 1973, or other Federal laws protecting the rights of children with disabilities, except that before the filing of a civil action under such laws seeking relief that is also available under this part, the procedures under subsections (f) and (g) shall be exhausted to the same extent as would be required had the action been brought under this part.

(m) TRANSFER OF PARENTAL RIGHTS AT AGE OF MAJORITY-

(1) IN GENERAL- A State that receives amounts from a grant under this part may provide that, when a child with a disability reaches the age of majority under State law (except for a child with a disability who has been determined to be incompetent under State law) --

(A) the public agency shall provide any notice required by this section to both the individual and the parents;

(B) all other rights accorded to parents under this part transfer to the child;

(C) the agency shall notify the individual and the parents of the transfer of rights; and

(D) all rights accorded to parents under this part transfer to children who are incarcerated in an adult or juvenile Federal, State, or local correctional institution.

(2) SPECIAL RULE- If, under State law, a child with a disability who has reached the age of majority under State law, who has not been determined to be incompetent, but who is determined not to have the ability to provide informed consent with respect to the educational program of the child, the State shall establish procedures for appointing the parent of the child, or if the parent is not available, another appropriate individual, to represent the educational interests of the child throughout the period of eligibility of the child under this part.

Appendix 3
IMPARTIAL DUE PROCESS HEARING-

(1) IN GENERAL- Whenever a complaint has been received under subsection (b)(6) or (k) of this section, the parents involved in such complaint shall have an opportunity for an impartial due process hearing, which shall be conducted by the State educational agency or by the local educational agency, as determined by State law or by the State educational agency.

(2) DISCLOSURE OF EVALUATIONS AND RECOMMENDATIONS-

(A) IN GENERAL- At least 5 business days prior to a hearing conducted pursuant to paragraph (1), each party shall disclose to all other parties all evaluations completed by that date and recommendations based on the offering party's evaluations that the party intends to use at the hearing.

(B) FAILURE TO DISCLOSE- A hearing officer may bar any party that fails to comply with subparagraph (A) from introducing the relevant evaluation or recommendation at the hearing without the consent of the other party.

(3) LIMITATION ON CONDUCT OF HEARING- A hearing conducted pursuant to paragraph (1) may not be conducted by an employee of the State educational agency or the local educational agency involved in the education or care of the child.

(g) APPEAL- If the hearing required by subsection (f) is conducted by a local educational agency, any party aggrieved by the findings and decision rendered in such a hearing may appeal such findings and decision to the State educational agency. Such agency shall conduct an impartial review of such decision. The officer conducting such review shall make an independent decision upon completion of such review.

(h) SAFEGUARDS- Any party to a hearing conducted pursuant to subsection (f) or (k), or an appeal conducted pursuant to subsection (g), shall be accorded --

(1) the right to be accompanied and advised by counsel and by individuals with special knowledge or training with respect to the problems of children with disabilities;

(2) the right to present evidence and confront, cross-examine, and compel the attendance of witnesses;

(3) the right to a written, or, at the option of the parents, electronic verbatim record of such hearing; and

(4) the right to written, or, at the option of the parents, electronic findings of fact and decisions (which findings and decisions shall be made available to the public consistent with the requirements of section 617(c) (relating to the confidentiality of data, information, and records) and shall also be transmitted to the advisory panel established pursuant to section 612(a)(21)).

(i) ADMINISTRATIVE PROCEDURES-

(1) IN GENERAL-

(A) DECISION MADE IN HEARING- A decision made in a hearing conducted pursuant to subsection (f) or (k) shall be final, except that any party involved in such hearing may appeal such decision under the provisions of subsection (g) and paragraph (2) of this subsection.

(B) DECISION MADE AT APPEAL- A decision made under subsection (g) shall be final, except that any party may bring an action under paragraph (2) of this subsection.

(2) RIGHT TO BRING CIVIL ACTION-

(A) IN GENERAL- Any party aggrieved by the findings and decision made under subsection (f) or (k) who does not have the right to an appeal under subsection (g), and any party aggrieved by the findings and decision under this subsection, shall have the right to bring a civil action with respect to the complaint presented pursuant to this section, which action may be brought in any State court of competent jurisdiction or in a district court of the United States without regard to the amount in controversy.

(B) ADDITIONAL REQUIREMENTS- In any action brought under this paragraph, the court --

(i) shall receive the records of the administrative proceedings;

(ii) shall hear additional evidence at the request of a party; and

(iii) basing its decision on the preponderance of the evidence, shall grant such relief as the court determines is appropriate.

(3) JURISDICTION OF DISTRICT COURTS; ATTORNEYS' FEES-

(A) IN GENERAL- The district courts of the United States shall have jurisdiction of actions brought under this section without regard to the amount in controversy.

(B) AWARD OF ATTORNEYS' FEES- In any action or proceeding brought under this section, the court, in its discretion, may award reasonable attorneys' fees as part of the costs to the parents of a child with a disability who is the prevailing party.

(C) DETERMINATION OF AMOUNT OF ATTORNEYS' FEES- Fees awarded under this paragraph shall be based on rates prevailing in the community in which the action or proceeding arose for the kind and quality of services furnished. No bonus or multiplier may be used in calculating the fees awarded under this subsection.

(D) PROHIBITION OF ATTORNEYS' FEES AND RELATED COSTS FOR CERTAIN SERVICES-

(i) Attorneys' fees may not be awarded and related costs may not be reimbursed in any action or proceeding under this section for services performed subsequent to the time of a written offer of settlement to a parent if --

(I) the offer is made within the time prescribed by Rule 68 of the Federal Rules of Civil Procedure or, in the case of an administrative proceeding, at any time more than 10 days before the proceeding begins;

(II) the offer is not accepted within 10 days; and

(III) the court or administrative hearing officer finds that the relief finally obtained by the parents is not more favorable to the parents than the offer of settlement.

(ii) Attorneys' fees may not be awarded relating to any meeting of the IEP Team unless such meeting is convened as a result of an administrative proceeding or judicial action, or, at the discretion of the State, for a mediation described in subsection (e) that is conducted prior to the filing of a complaint under subsection (b)(6) or (k) of this section.

(E) EXCEPTION TO PROHIBITION ON ATTORNEYS' FEES AND RELATED COSTS- Notwithstanding subparagraph (D), an award of attorneys' fees and related costs may be made to a parent who is the prevailing party and who was substantially justified in rejecting the settlement offer.

(F) REDUCTION IN AMOUNT OF ATTORNEYS' FEES- Except as provided in subparagraph (G), whenever the court finds that --

(i) the parent, during the course of the action or proceeding, unreasonably protracted the final resolution of the controversy;

(ii) the amount of the attorneys' fees otherwise authorized to be awarded unreasonably exceeds the hourly rate prevailing in the community for similar services by attorneys of reasonably comparable skill, reputation, and experience;

(iii) the time spent and legal services furnished were excessive considering the nature of the action or proceeding; or

(iv) the attorney representing the parent did not provide to the school district the appropriate information in the due process complaint in accordance with subsection (b)(7); the court shall reduce, accordingly, the amount of the attorneys' fees awarded under this section.

(G) EXCEPTION TO REDUCTION IN AMOUNT OF ATTORNEYS' FEES- The provisions of subparagraph (F) shall not apply in any action or proceeding if the court finds that the State or local educational agency unreasonably protracted the final resolution of the action or proceeding or there was a violation of this section.

(j) MAINTENANCE OF CURRENT EDUCATIONAL PLACEMENT- Except as provided in subsection (k)(7), during the pendency of any proceedings conducted pursuant to this section, unless the

State or local educational agency and the parents otherwise agree, the child shall remain in the then-current educational placement of such child, or, if applying for initial admission to a public school, shall, with the consent of the parents, be placed in the public school program until all such proceedings have been completed.

ABOUT THE AUTHOR

Carolyn Lampman Brubaker is the award-winning author of seven historical fiction novels, numerous articles and the screenplay for an educational video. In her other life, she is a twenty-eight year veteran of the teaching profession. She lives in a small town in Wyoming with her husband, two children and a Welsh Corgi.

For your reading pleasure, we welcome you to visit our web bookstore

WHISKEY CREEK PRESS

www.whiskeycreekpress.com